USING ANNUAL EDITIONS FOR TEACHING

Introduction

It has often been noted that we are living in the middle of an information revolution. For more than a decade, that revolution has had an effect on teaching and learning. Where once a student could grasp the basic tenets of a discipline by studying a textbook developed two or three years prior to its publication and actually used by the student for some five years after that, today new perspectives are constantly updating those basic tenets and are at times fundamentally challenging them.

Teachers are frequently hard-pressed to keep up with advances in their fields. Often their attempts to keep their students informed and aware are limited by the difficulty of making new materials available. Students line up at reserve desks of libraries for an insufficient handful of reprint articles, or lack the patience to research a bibliography of suggested article titles a teacher might provide. As a result, students often miss one of the most valuable components of such a teaching effort: the opportunity to witness their field of study in process, as an alive and changing field. Moreover, they miss the opportunity to observe the practical applications of ideas and theories their basic texts provide.

The *ANNUAL EDITIONS* series is designed to remedy this problem. Each of its more than forty titles is developed and regularly updated by an educator in the field. Each title has an average of fifty articles culled from a broad spectrum of sources and provides both an overview and an intensive examination of particular topic areas in the field of study. The books are grouped in focus sections and cross-referenced according to subject and topic. The variety, scope, and breadth of the books in the *ANNUAL EDITIONS* series make them invaluable for correcting the blind spots that frequently occur in curriculum design.

The *ANNUAL EDITIONS* books can be integrated into a course curriculum in a variety of ways:

They can be used as a text support. Here, a selection of articles might be used on a weekly basis in support of basic material covered in a textbook. Four or five articles per week could serve to illustrate or reinforce some basic theoretical points.

They can be used as supplemental texts. The material in a basic textbook can be enhanced with the addition of interesting and effective supplemental readings. The *ANNUAL EDITIONS* comprehensive topic guides and indexes can easily be used to expand any text.

They can be used as basic texts. Although the *ANNUAL EDITIONS* books are made up largely of readings, each book provides a theoretical overview in the form of basic articles in the field. These articles serve as a framework for examining and understanding the discipline, while companion articles make clear the implementation of that framework. With this, the teacher has the opportunity to generate a "hands on" sense of the discipline.

In whatever way they are used, the *ANNUAL EDITIONS* books provide a valuable resource to the study of a discipline.

SOME GENERAL REMARKS

The basic need of both teacher and student is to have useful information readily accessible. Beyond this, the objectives for both the teaching and the study of such information are:

1. To assure comprehension of the material and to integrate it with the basic tenets of the field it represents.

2. To use comprehension of that material as a vehicle for critical thinking, reasoning, and effective argument.

Information is valueless unless it is put to use: otherwise it becomes mere data. To use information most effectively it should be taken as an instrument for understanding. The process of this utilization works on a number of incremental levels. Information can be:

> absorbed (read),
> comprehended or reinforced,
> discussed,
> argued in reasoned fashion,
> written about, and
> integrated with similar and contrasting information.

Though all of this might beg the obvious to the reader, it is part and parcel of the critical thinking used in developing the *Annual Editions Instructor's Resource Guides,* teaching guides for the use of *ANNUAL EDITIONS* texts.

DEVELOPING THE STUDENT'S POWERS OF CRITICAL THINKING WITH *ANNUAL EDITIONS*

The development of critical and analytical thinking is the key to the understanding and use of information. It is what allows the student to discuss and argue points of opinion and points of fact. It is the basis for the student's formation of independent ideas. Once formed, these ideas can be written about and integrated with both similar and contrasting information.

The editors of the *ANNUAL EDITIONS* series and companion *Annual Editions Instructor's Resource Guides* have noted a number of cognitive skills involved in critical thinking that are fundamentally interrelated. They have served as criteria in the development of *Annual Editions Instructor's Resource Guides* and are grounded in a pedagogical sense of the equipment students need to evaluate what they have read. Here are a number of ideas and approaches that illustrate how material from *ANNUAL EDITIONS* can be used to teach critical thinking skills.

ELEMENTS OF CRITICAL THINKING

- Differentiating between fact and opinion
- Recognizing and evaluating author bias and rhetoric
- Determining cause-and-effect relationships
- Determining the accuracy and completeness of information presented
- Recognizing logical fallacies and faulty reasoning
- Comparing and contrasting information and points of view
- Developing inferential skills
- Making judgments and drawing logical conclusions

Differentiating Between Fact and Opinion

A *fact* is a statement that can be proven true by other verifiable facts. An *opinion* is a statement of a person's feelings or impressions. The articles in the *ANNUAL EDITIONS* books are ideally suited to develop the ability to differentiate between statements of fact and statements of opinion. For example, students reading an article on foreign policy in *Annual Editions: World Politics* will come across a number of both facts and opinions. After reading the article, the students might be asked to set down three statements of fact and three of opinion. Guidelines might be:

> What externally verifiable information is presented that makes this statement true, or factual?

W9-BAO-340

How does the author differentiate between the interpretation of information and the presentation of factual data?

Discussion of the subject might be encouraged by the following:

What rules or techniques can be used to identify statements of fact? Of opinion?

Can a statement contain both fact and opinion?

Can some opinions be considered reliable? Why?

Recognizing and Evaluating Author Bias and Rhetoric

Because they contain a number of articles on related topics, the *ANNUAL EDITIONS* books offer a unique opportunity to analyze and evaluate author bias and the author's use of rhetorical ploys and techniques. Upon reading the article in question, the following may be asked:

What qualifications does the author have for writing on this subject? (What are the qualifications of the individuals the author quotes?)

When and where was this article first published? Does this information affect the credibility of the article?

What do you think the author wants his/her readers to think or do?

Determining Cause-and-Effect Relationships

Through attentive reading of an article, a student may come to understand that one situation of determinable fact may generate a second, fundamentally related situation. As an example, articles in *Annual Editions: Health* may take up the effect of smoking and consumption of alcohol on the body. In an attempt to clarify the cause-and-effect relationship, questions such as the following might be asked in discussion:

What are the effects of alcohol on the liver?

Can the combination of alcohol and cigarettes increase the risk of acquiring diseases? What diseases?

What effects on diet does alcohol consumption have?

Similar questions could just as easily be put to world affairs, psychology, or government. The issue here is of determining factual data and then of determining its effect in the real-world order.

Determining the Accuracy and Completeness of Information Presented

Once fact and opinion have been differentiated, author bias known, and a rudimentary understanding of cause-and-effect relationships examined, it must be determined if the information presented is complete and accurate. Is more information needed?

The *ANNUAL EDITIONS* books provide the student with the opportunity to examine articles in terms of a broader spectrum of fact and opinion. Articles within a particular topic area may give the student an opportunity to evaluate the bias of one article in the face of another. It may also give the student a chance to examine divergent opinions gleaned from the same data. For example, a section on the environmental effects of acid rain presented in *Annual Editions: Environment* may include a number of articles written by both Canadian and American authors. The question that might be put before a student is whether each article provides enough information for an unbiased assessment of the situation. Questions that might be offered in discussion of a group of articles on the subject are:

What facts do all the articles in the discussion use?

What important facts are used in some of the articles, but not in all of them?

What sources could be used to check the information presented in each of the articles?

Recognizing Logical Fallacies and Faulty Reasoning

Critical thinking requires the ability to recognize faulty logic. Here are seven major examples of fallacies of reasoning that students should be able to recognize. Notice that several of them are variations of the criteria for critical thinking. The fallacies are:

1. Incorrect assumption of cause/effect relationship.
   For example: Every time I wash my car, it rains; therefore, if I wash my car, it will rain.
2. Inaccurate or distorted use of the interpretation of numerical statistical information.
   For example: Lowering of the speed limit on highways to 55 mph results in fewer traffic fatalities. (Such information should be checked against the number of people using the highways since the institution of such laws. Are there now fewer people driving?)
3. Faulty analogy, comparison carried too far, or comparison of things that have nothing in common.
   For example: Apples and oranges are both fruit and grow on trees; therefore, apples and oranges taste the same.
4. Oversimplification. Potentially relevant information is ignored in order to make a point.
   For example: The majority of voters in the United States are Democrats; therefore, Democratic candidates will win every election.
5. Stereotyping. People or objects are lumped together under simplistic labels.
   For example: Hispanic Americans all speak Spanish; therefore, Spanish language advertising will appeal to all of them.
6. Ignoring the question. Digression, obfuscation, or similar techniques are used to avoid answering a question.
   For example: When asked about a tax increase possibility, a senator replies, "I have always met the obligations I have to those I represent."
7. Faulty generalization. A judgment is based on insufficient evidence.
   For example: Ducks and geese migrate south for the winter; therefore, all waterfowl migrate south for the winter.

Comparing and Contrasting Information and Points of View

To compare and contrast, students must have a wide variety of material at hand. The *ANNUAL EDITIONS* series identifies differences and similarities among the facts, opinions, purposes, and points of view in a number of articles related to a single topic. By comparing and contrasting, students can identify facts and draw conclusions more readily.

Developing Inferential Skills

Because of the broad variety of material presented by the *ANNUAL EDITIONS* series, the student can take up a line of argument from one article and apply it to another. A discussion guideline for this is:

In article A, the author claims that the reason for the current state of affairs was the result of X, Y, and Z. If that has been proven false, how do those findings affect the related argument in article B?

Making Judgments and Drawing Logical Conclusions

Making judgments and drawing logical conclusions require the implementation of all the previously examined critical-thinking skills. Questions such as the following can help students successfully grasp the information that has been presented to them:

> What are the conclusions drawn by the author of this article?
>
> Do you agree or disagree with the author's conclusions?
>
> What other conclusion is it possible to draw from the same information?
>
> What other information might it be important to know before making any judgment of the value and import of this article?

After students have evaluated the information presented in articles, a sample form may be presented (page 6). This form is intended as an idea starter. *ANNUAL EDITIONS* users have adapted this basic form to a wide range of instructional situations and needs. This form requires the students to summarize the article and briefly analyze what they have read. The completed form can then be used as a starting point for class discussions, expanded into a larger writing activity, or used to check on student comprehension of the reading. Try variations of the form in your classroom.

THE ANNUAL EDITIONS INSTRUCTOR'S RESOURCE GUIDES—DESIGN AND USE

Following along the lines of critical thinking that the *ANNUAL EDITIONS* series develops, the *Annual Editions Instructor's Resource Guides* have been designed to enhance and reinforce both the student's and the teacher's understanding and use of *ANNUAL EDITIONS* materials in the classrooms. The *Annual Editions Instructor's Resource Guides* have two main components:

> **Guidelines** on using the particular text in the classroom. These have been developed by the editors of the particular *ANNUAL EDITIONS* text and are based on actual usage of the text in teaching situations. Where possible, helpful examples are provided that are geared toward the use of specific *ANNUAL EDITIONS* titles in teaching situations.
>
> **The question bank** for use in discussion and testing of issues. This is the largest component and can be used variously as a springboard for discussion, as a source for writing questions, as a test bank for multiple choice questions, and as a general glossary of key terms. It can serve to reinforce comprehension of the material in an *ANNUAL EDITIONS* text and as a spur to critical thinking.

The **question bank** is the most important component of the *Annual Editions Instructor's Resource Guides* and deserves further analysis. The following expands on this element.

THE QUESTION BANK FORMAT

The question bank is divided into four sections:

> **Article Summary.**
> **Key Terms and Topics.**
> **Critical Analysis.**
> **General Questions** that are designed to:
> note author bias;
> open larger issues; and
> relate the article to trends in the field.

ARTICLE SUMMARY

This includes a brief precis of the material discussed in the article. It makes note of the style and tone of the article as well as its format and content, and is both synoptic and evaluative. The summary highlights the main issues and arguments, and notes the author's point of view and conclusion. For example: "A measured and scholarly article concerning the effect of _____ on _____, illustrated with many graphs. The author's three central claims are..." or "A general-interest piece marking broad trends and developments in the field of _____. Its main examples are developed from events in _____, _____, and _____. The author holds that..."

KEY TERMS AND TOPICS

This section highlights a number of key topics, phrases, or lines of argument with reference to their use in the text. Special attention is paid to how key phrases from the field are used in the context of the particular article. For example, from *Annual Editions: Marketing*:

> *Target Marketing* directing a consumer product toward a particular class, age group, or region.
> *Demographics* the process of researching the tastes and consumer tendencies of certain social groups.
> *Analysis-Paralysis* the tendency to over-research a particular market and not take entrepreneurial risks.
> *Marketing Bureaucracy* a non-entrepreneurial class of marketers that inhibits business risk-taking.

The words or phrases chosen are defined as they are used in the text so that some of the authorial perspective, or bias, is able to show itself. It is conceivable that the same words may be used differently in another article, and so might be listed again.

CRITICAL ANALYSIS

This section is designed as multiple choice and true/false questions and focuses on the development of "test bank" questions to evaluate a student's comprehension of the article under discussion.

Multiple Choice Questions

There are an average of four multiple choice questions per article, each with four possible or viable choices developed from the article itself. For example, from *Annual Editions: Psychology*:

> B.F. Skinner's *Beyond Freedom and Dignity*, "astounded the psychological community," according to the article, by:
> a. claiming that man can improve himself by developing his own creativity.
> b. stating that "free will" is the most important issue in psychology today.
> *c. claiming that man would be better off in a controlled society of rewards and punishments.
> d. holding that behavior should be modified by the use of implanted electrodes and psychotropic drugs.

The proper answer (c) is taken from a line presented in the text. Similarly, each of the other answer options is also taken from text material. The idea is that the multiple choice question is a vehicle for reviewing lines of argument in the article at hand and for reinforcing comprehension of the critical-thinking aspects of the idea it presents.

Multiple choice questions may also be structured to present the correct answer by negative exclusion. For example, from *Annual Editions: Marketing*:

ANNUAL EDITIONS ARTICLE REPORT

STUDENT NAME: _____ DATE: _____

TITLE AND NUMBER OF ARTICLE: _____

BRIEFLY STATE THE MAIN IDEA OF THIS ARTICLE: _____

_____

_____

_____

_____

LIST THREE IMPORTANT FACTS THAT THE AUTHOR USES TO SUPPORT THE MAIN IDEA:

_____

_____

_____

_____

_____

_____

WHAT INFORMATION OR IDEAS DISCUSSED IN THIS ARTICLE ARE ALSO DISCUSSED IN YOUR TEXTBOOK? PLEASE LIST TEXTBOOK CHAPTERS AND PAGE NUMBERS:

_____

_____

_____

_____

_____

_____

LIST ANY EXAMPLES OF BIAS OR FAULTY REASONING THAT YOU FOUND IN THE ARTICLE:

_____

_____

_____

_____

_____

This form is intended as an idea starter. *ANNUAL EDITIONS* users have adapted this basic form to a wide range of instructional situations and needs.

According to Levitt's "The Globalization of Markets," Hoover Ltd's troubles with marketing automatic laundry equipment in Western Europe developed from all the following *except:*

a. insufficient demand in the home market and low European exports.
b. customizing the product to meet national preference standards.
c. individual country tariffs.
*d. the company's efforts to standardize the product.

The choices, as well as the question, are strongly tied to the article. The choice options are virtually quoted from the text.

True/False Questions

There are an average of two true/false questions per article. The questions are worded similarly to statements in the articles and reinforce close careful reading of the articles.

GENERAL QUESTIONS

These questions fall into three specific areas, with each of the three categories designed to meet a specific teaching need.

1. Questions designed to *note author bias* provide a way to lead the student along the lines of the author's argument in the interest of developing both a sense of the author's reasoning process and the student's evaluative, logical, and inferential skills. Lines of response are provided for each question. For example, from *Annual Editions: Marketing:*

> The author claims that innovative marketing efforts would have "low priority in management budgets." What other evidence does he provide to lead you to think this might be the case? *(ideas: corporations, according to the author, tend to devise means of controlling assets and generally avoid issues of how marketing might be used in tandem with research and development projects; the author claims that venture capital ideas get lost in corporate bureaucracy)*

2. Questions designed to *open larger issues.* These are largely for discussion value. In certain articles, provocative ideas are generated that deserve attention both within and without the framework of the course under study. Here the question takes up the specific point in the text *and* moves on to broader issues. The idea is to invite speculative responses. Along with the question, a few ideas are provided as guidelines for how discussion might develop. In this way, a number of guideline criteria for developing critical thinking are met. For example, from *Annual Editions: Environment:*

> Erik Eckholm, in "Human Wants and Misused Lands," points out that rangeland degradation results from overgrazing and the depletion of tree cover for fuel and building materials. What Third World development trends contribute to this kind of desertification? Do you think that rangeland degradation could be a problem in the rest of the world? *(trends: urbanization and increased need for fuel and building materials, compression of herdsmen into smaller areas by spread of settled farming; argument on the rest of the world: hinges on whether the population growth, rising costs of renewable fuel sources, and greater demand for food crops are considered affordable)*

3. Questions designed to *relate the article to trends in the field* reinforce a broad overview of article material and provide the means for the student to integrate ideas of the article with the general themes of the section of the *ANNUAL EDITIONS* text in which the article appears, or with the broader issues of the course or discipline. These questions are set up to compel the student to argue from points made in the text, and are often the best questions for use in written test material. For example, from *Annual Editions: Psychology:*

> Evaluate the use of the disorder hypoglycemia as the basis of defense in criminal prosecution as it is explained in the article, "Brain Triggers." Is it a convincing case? *(lines of response: hypoglycemia, or critically low blood sugar, can trigger nervousness and even irrational behavior; unconsciousness can also occur; the issue is whether such activity might be considered the basis for defending anti-social behavior; the student might compare and contrast other disorders with hypoglycemia: can they be placed on a spectrum?)*

USING THE QUESTION BANK

Throughout the question bank, the basic tenets of critical thinking are implemented both as criteria for the formation of questions and as the basis for responding to them. With a basic understanding of the format of the *Annual Editions Instructor's Resource Guides* (IRG) question bank, the instructor can begin to see the range of possibilities for its use:

> For example, the **article summaries** may be used by the instructor as guidelines for the selection of articles to assign his or her class. They may just as easily be used as a shorthand reference in the discussion preparation or as a reference in testing for article comprehension.

> **Key terms and topics** may be used in glossary fashion to reinforce student comprehension through testing, or to promote discussion of the basic concepts the terms represent. They may also serve in broader discussions of authorial slant or bias. In this way, they can help the student to evaluate the article as a whole.

> While the **critical analysis** multiple choice questions are clearly best used in testing, their companion Topic Identification/Author Strategy questions can be used in a number of ways. Most significantly, they can be used to promote critical thinking and reasoning through discussion and written evaluation.

> Similarly, the **general questions** that are designed to "note author bias," the questions designed to "relate the article to trends in the field," and the questions designed to "open larger issues" can be used either for essay or discussion. They may also serve as good reading notes for the student in need of a more structured and personalized reinforcement. Finally, they can serve as guidelines to the teacher interested in developing his or her own questions along similar lines.

The *Annual Editions Instructor's Resource Guides* provide both teacher and student with new opportunities to explore materials already at hand. At the same time, the guides provide ideas for examining, in detail, other ideas that various media in their fields present.

1. THE NECESSARY RESTRUCTURING OF SPECIAL AND REGULAR EDUCATION,
MAYNARD C. REYNOLDS, MARGARET C. WANG, AND HERBERT J. WALBERG   **AE p. 6**

ARTICLE SUMMARY

Three scholars contend that there are major flaws in the way special eduation is currently categorized. They illustrate a lack of consistency in the way labels are applied from a broad base of research. They endorse efforts to create more valid, more reliable models without undermining the rights of handicapped children guaranteed by PL 94-142.

KEY TERMS AND TOPICS

Special Education education for children who deviate from the norm to the extent that they require special services, facilities, curricula, instructional materials, educational procedures, or special teaching competencies.

Educational Testing and Labeling critical examination of the sensory, perceptual and cognitive abilities of a child by qualitative and/or quantitative means in order to assign the child to a category for educational placement.

Valid capable of testing or measuring what it is supposed to measure.

Reliable trustworthy of yielding consistent judgments under varying conditions of testing or measurement.

PL 94-142 the Education for All Handicapped Children Act of the USA which guarantees free and appropriate education for all handicapped children between the ages of 3 and 18.

CRITICAL ANALYSIS

Multiple Choice Questions

1. According to "The Necessary Restructuring of Special and Regular Education," itinerant school psychologists and social workers spend most of their in-school time working with children who are:
   a. poorly motivated to achieve up to their ability levels.
   *b. enrolled in special education programs.
   c. suffering from neglect or abuse.
   d. grieving due to family problems.
2. According to "The Necessary Restructuring of Special and Regular Education," special educational services for which category of exceptionality have shown the largest growth in recent years?
   a. mentally retarded.
   b. emotionally disabled.
   *c. learning disabled.
   d. hearing impaired.
3. The authors of "The Necessary Restructuring of Special and Regular Education" favor collaboration of federal, state and local governments to support more ___ forms of education for students with special needs.
   a. compensatory
   b. remedial
   c. segregated
   *d. integrated

True/False Questions

4. Requirements for some form of special educational services are much higher for children who were born with low birth weight than they are for children who were born at normal birth weight, according to "The Necessary Restructuring of Special and Regular Education." (T)
5. The "Rights Without Labels" statement in "The Necessary Restructuring of Special and Regular Education" proposes that students with special needs should be barred from regular classroom settings. (F)

GENERAL QUESTIONS

6. The authors of "The Necessary Restructuring of Special and Regular Education" believe that the number and the proportion of children having special needs will continue to rise over the next several years. What are some of the reasons they give for this belief?
   (higher fertility rate among women of low income levels, children in poverty more frequently judged to be in need of special services, low birth weight infants more frequently in need of special educational services, general increase in the school-age population)
7. What might be the effects on normal children of a restructuring of special education which places more children with special needs in regular classrooms, according to "The Necessary Restructuring of Special and Regular Education"?
   (**pro:** *more interaction between normal children and exceptional children; more understanding of, and compassion for, exceptional children by normal children; less fear of the unknown/special education;* **con:** *less teacher time directed to their specific academic needs; fewer group lessons*)
8. In what ways will the series of pilot projects proposed by the authors of "The Necessary Restructuring of Special and Regular Education" advance the goal of mainstreaming? In what ways might they hinder the goal of mainstreaming?
   (**advance:** *more integrated classrooms; curriculum-based identification systems; building-based collaboration;* **hinder:** *increased stresses on students and teachers unless class size is limited*)

2. WHERE IS SPECIAL EDUCATION FOR STUDENTS WITH HIGH PREVALENCE HANDICAPS GOING?
BOB ALGOZZINE AND LORI KORINEK   **AE p. 13**

ARTICLE SUMMARY

This article is a study of trends in the proportion of students with varieties of handicaps who are receiving special educational services. The data is broken down by state and region and the more rapidly growing categories are identified.

KEY TERMS AND TOPICS

Prevalence Estimate the number of handicapped students counted at any given time.

High Prevalence Handicaps the most numerous categories: learning disabled, speech impaired, mentally retarded, and emotionally disturbed.

CRITICAL ANALYSIS

Multiple Choice Questions

1. PL 94-142 was signed into law by which US president and in what year, according to "Where Is Special Education for Students with High Prevalence Handicaps Going?"
   a. Richard Nixon, 1972.
   *b. Gerald Ford, 1975.
   c. Jimmy Carter, 1978.
   d. Ronald Reagan, 1981.
2. As mentioned in "Where Is Special Education for Students with High Prevalence Handicaps Going?" all of the following are high prevalence handicaps *except:*
   *a. deaf and hearing impaired.
   b. speech impaired.
   c. emotionally disabled.
   d. learning disabled.
3. The authors of "Where Is Special Education for Students with High Prevalence Handicaps Going?" feel that all of the following factors except ___ create problems of overpopulated special education classes.
   a. social factors
   b. economic factors
   *c. religious factors
   d. political factors

True/False Questions

4. According to "Where Is Special Education for Students with High Prevalence Handicaps Going?" the federal government recognizes 10 categories of handicapping conditions under

which children are eligible for special educational services under PL 94-142. (T)

5. The authors of "Where Is Special Education for Students with High Prevalence Handicaps Going?" believe that more efforts to define concepts, and to define the conditions now referred to as hidden handicaps, will solve the problem of deciding who is eligible for special education. (F)

GENERAL QUESTIONS

6. What are some of the arguments advanced by the authors of "Where Is Special Education for Students with High Prevalence Handicaps Going?" to support the notion that there are not really more learning disabled than mentally retarded children today, but that more students are simply classified as LD than as MR?
(changed definitions of LD and MR; LD easier to find today with new diagnostic tools and strategies; more money available for LD classes; greater social desirability of LD label)

7. If the learning disability category continues to grow at the rate of 3% of the special education population a year, how must teacher preparation programs be changed to meet the needs of the increased LD population, according to "Where Is Special Education for Students with High Prevalence Handicaps Going?"
(more courses on how to teach LD students; more differentiation between types of LD; separation of underachievers from LD; more emphasis on developing individualized education programs)

8. According to "Where Is Special Education for Students with High Prevalence Handicaps Going?" what positive and what negative conclusions could be drawn from the data presented on changes in the proportion of handicapped students in various categories?
(positive: *increasingly effective specialized education; improved diagnostic strategies for learning disabled; prevention and alleviation of mental retardation through medicine, early intervention, parent programs, and technology.* **negative:** *an increasingly ineffective system not based on student's needs; impact of social, political, legal, and economic factors on the categorization process; more profitable and socially desirable to find more learning disabled and fewer retarded students)*

3. THE *TATRO* CASE: WHO GETS WHAT AND WHY, STANLEY J. VITELLO   AE p. 19

ARTICLE SUMMARY

This article presents a scholarly discussion of the second special education case decided by the US Supreme Court: *Tatro v. State of Texas.* The case provides some criteria for determining which related services are required under PL 94-142. These criteria are discussed in relation to other recent special education cases.

KEY TERMS AND TOPICS

Related Supportive Services any services that permit an exceptional child to obtain access to education, remain at school during the day, and to benefit from the educational program.
Least Restrictive Environment an educational setting for an exceptional child which comes as close as possible to a regular classroom, or is a regular classroom.

CRITICAL ANALYSIS

Multiple Choice Questions

1. According to "The *Tatro* Case," Amber Tatro, the subject of the *Tatro v. State of Texas* lawsuit disputing the school's responsibility for a catheterization procedure, had which of the following illnesses?
   a. cystic fibrosis.
   *b. spina bifida.
   c. polio.
   d. muscular dystrophy.

2. The Supreme Court decision, as explained in "The *Tatro* Case," was that catheterization is a related supportive service required for children in need:
   a. of early childhood centers.
   b. of special schools.
   c. of schools with a physician on their staff.
   *d. of any school.

3. According to "The *Tatro* Case," a school does not have to perform a life support service for a child if that service:
   *a. need not be performed during the school day.
   b. assists the child to benefit from special education.
   c. is for diagnostic and evaluation purposes.
   d. must be performed by a school nurse, school social worker, or other licensed staff member.

True/False Questions

4. As detailed in "The *Tatro* Case," the Texas district court, Court of Appeals, and Supreme Court were all in agreement on the *Tatro* decision on catheterization. (F)

5. Whether or not a particular medical service fits the definition of a related supportive service is determined by who provides the service, not the type of service per se, according to "The *Tatro* Case." (T)

GENERAL QUESTIONS

6. The author of "The *Tatro* Case" cited decisions in a number of lower courts which were consistent with the guidelines on related supportive services established by the *Tatro* case. What are some of these specific services ruled related supportive services by the lower courts?
(air-conditioned classroom; tracheotomy tube insertion; transportation from school to bus and from bus to school; psychiatric counseling)

7. Many schools do not have a school nurse on staff. According to "The *Tatro* Case," what could a school do if a child requiring catheterization enrolled?
(hire a school nurse; contract to have an itinerant school nurse visit the school once daily; hire a nurse's aide or medic licensed to do catheterization; have an employed staff member become trained and licensed to perform catheterization)

8. PL 94-142 not only requires a free and appropriate education with related services to meet each exceptional child's unique needs but also mandates that the education should be in the least restrictive environment compatible with the handicap. As explained in "The *Tatro* Case," what does this mean for the educational program of teachers preparing to teach regular classes?
(more courses on exceptional conditions; more emphasis on developing individualized education programs; more flexibility in changing lesson plans to accommodate children with unique needs; willingness to perform some non-physician-administered medical services for children)

4. LESSONS FROM MAINSTREAMING, STEPHANIE LYNN   AE p. 22

ARTICLE SUMMARY

This article is an informed description of one mainstreamed school with a disproportionately large concentration of orthopedically handicapped children. The author discusses the pros and cons of having exceptional children in magnet schools with several similarly handicapped children versus being mainstreamed in schools closer to their own homes.

KEY TERMS AND TOPICS

Mainstreaming the placement of exceptional children in regular classrooms whenever possible, or for as long as possible each day.
Cerebral Palsy condition of some muscular spasticity or paralysis due to a lesion of the brain, usually sustained close to birth.

Orthopedic Handicap disability related to some deformity of the skeletal system or the muscles supporting it.
Barrier-Free Schools schools with ramps, wide doorways, special lavatories and other appliances which make them fully accessible to persons in wheelchairs.

CRITICAL ANALYSIS
Multiple Choice Questions

1. A problem was presented in "Lessons from Mainstreaming." Erik preferred his regular class but funding laws required that he spend 60% of each day in special education. The school resolved the problem by:
    a. transferring him to another school.
    b. putting him in a full-time special class.
    *c. letting his regular teacher and his special-ed teacher team teach.
    d. sacrificing the funds for his special-ed so he could remain in a regular class.
2. The school described in "Lessons from Mainstreaming," P.S. 279 of Brooklyn, N.Y., was a magnet school for a large number of ___ handicapped students.
    *a. orthopedically
    b. visually
    c. emotionally
    d. speech/language
3. According to "Lessons from Mainstreaming," what is the future of magnet schools such as P.S. 279 in Brooklyn, N.Y.?
    a. they will be closed due to underenrollment.
    *b. they will be phased out to comply with PL 94-142.
    c. they will be expanded to serve more exceptional children.
    d. they will serve as models for thousands of new magnet schools now under construction.

True/False Questions

4. According to "Lessons from Mainstreaming," P.S. 279 in Brooklyn, N.Y., believed that it was useful to make distinctions between handicapped and nonhandicapped students. (F)
5. According to "Lessons from Mainstreaming," all public schools need not be barrier-free as long as one barrier-free magnet school exists in a school district to serve the needs of handicapped students. (F)

GENERAL QUESTIONS

6. In "Lessons from Mainstreaming," P.S. 279 of Brooklyn, N.Y., was featured. This school had large numbers of handicapped students and a greater-than-usual number of supportive service personnel beyond regular and special-education teachers. Who were some of these extra staff members?
    (health coordinator; guidance counselor; nurses' aides; health paraprofessionals; occupational therapists; physical therapists)
7. In the article, "Lessons from Mainstreaming," the author quotes the director of an Educational Research Center as stating, "When a school provides an environment that is inclusive of students with differences, then having kids who are different in large numbers can make them the norm rather than the exception." What are other advantages of having large numbers of exceptional students in one school? What are some disadvantages?
    (advantages: *built-in support system for each exceptional child; staff knowledgeable about special needs of handicapped;* **disadvantages:** *need more special staff to provide support services for handicapped; long bus rides to bring handicapped to magnet school; handicapped students do not get to know children in their own neighborhood school)*
8. Will the full implementation of PL 94-142's mainstreaming concept be more or less expensive to each neighborhood school, according to "Lessons from Mainstreaming"?
    (more expensive: *must be constructed barrier-free; must have staff to provide supportive services;* **less expensive:** *do not have to bus students to distant special schools; can teach more handicapped students in regular classrooms)*

5. "IT'LL BE A CHALLENGE!": MANAGING EMOTIONAL STRESS IN TEACHING DISABLED CHILDREN,
BARBARA PALM WHITE AND MICHAEL A. PHAIR
AE p. 26

ARTICLE SUMMARY

This article presents a semi-personal account of several emotional reactions experienced while teaching mainstreamed exceptional children. Each emotion is explored in terms of its negative effects and ways to minimize its occurrence. The authors hold that honestly looking at emotions benefit both personal and professional skills.

KEY TERMS AND TOPICS

Denial avoidance of a problem by overlooking it or pretending it does not exist.
Defensiveness blocking ideas from others or viewing them as veiled criticism.
Fatalism a perspective of the overwhelming hopelessness of a situation.

CRITICAL ANALYSIS
Multiple Choice Questions

1. According to "It'll Be a Challenge!" "if only..." comments such as if only I knew more, if only I'd worked harder, etc., are signals of the presence of the negative emotion of:
    a. denial.
    b. overprotection.
    c. fatalism.
    *d. guilt.
2. The authors of "It'll Be a Challenge!" suggest which of the following as a way of overcoming sorrow over a child's disabilities?
    a. share the information with associates.
    b. reaffirm one's commitment to a career in education.
    *c. record the child's every success, however small.
    d. examine the sorrow to see if it is caused by something else.
3. The authors of "It'll Be a Challenge!" suggest that concentrating on the ___ and things that ___ be controlled helps to overcome fatalism.
    *a. present; can
    b. present; cannot
    c. past; can
    d. future; cannot

True/False Questions

4. The authors of "It'll Be a Challenge!" have suggested ways for educators to channel their thinking into eight progressively more relaxed states in order to serve children better. (F)
5. According to "It'll Be a Challenge!" overlooking, denying, or avoiding the reality of a child's disabilities will lead to an increased sense of guilt as a teacher. (T)

GENERAL QUESTIONS

6. The authors of "It'll Be a Challenge!" presented 11 negative emotions and ways in which to overcome them in order to be more effective as a teacher. Name a few of the negative emotions described in the article.
    (denial, sadness, anger, guilt, fear, overprotection, defensiveness, jealousy/competition, frustration, exhaustion, fatalism)
7. As related in "It'll Be a Challenge!" what are some of the fears which teachers of disabled children may experience related to the child, and some of the fears they may experience related to themselves?
    (child: *fear that he or she may die, get worse, hurt self; fear that he or she may hurt another child; fear that he or she may hurt teacher;* **self:** *fear of inadequacy as teacher; fear of*

inability to cope; fear of parents' responses; fear of what others think)

8. Burnout is a common phenomenon among school teachers and is especially prevalent among teachers of exceptional children. According to "It'll Be a Challenge!" what precautions should special-education teachers take to help prevent burnout?
(frequent short breaks during school day; non-break time set aside during school day for record keeping and planning; no requests to work overtime or during vacations and weekends; encourage pursuit of different interests or hobbies while away from work)

6. PRACTICAL SUGGESTIONS FOR PLANNING AND CONDUCTING PARENT CONFERENCES,
BARRIE JO PRICE AND GEORGE E. MARSH II
AE p. 31

ARTICLE SUMMARY

This article is a general interest piece which presents suggestions for communicating with parents which can easily be incorporated into teacher preparation courses. The authors develop ideas for planning, conducting, terminating and following up on parent-teacher conferences. Their suggestions are aimed at reducing the anxiety felt by both teachers and parents surrounding such meetings.

KEY TERMS AND TOPICS

Due Process Hearings meetings to review legal procedures to ensure that an individual's constitutional rights are served and protected.
Parent-Teacher Conferences meetings between parents and teachers to share and learn from each other about the student's performance and behavior in order to maximize the educational experience.
Individualized Education Program (IEP) an annually updated plan for the education of every handicapped student which includes services to be delivered and procedures by which the outcome will be evaluated.

CRITICAL ANALYSIS
Multiple Choice Questions

1. According to "Practical Suggestions for Planning and Conducting Parent Conferences," PL 94-142 requires interaction between parents and their handicapped child's school teacher for the purpose of:
   a. planning a payment of service fees schedule.
   b. IQ testing of parents as a supplement to the child's cognitive evaluation.
   c. supplying referral data from physicians, psychiatrists and other professionals.
   *d. developing an individualized education plan.
2. All of the following were recommended ways to prepare for a parent-teacher conference by the authors of "Practical Suggestions for Planning and Conducting Parent Conferences" *except:*
   a. have samples of student's work available to show parents.
   b. review the student's test data, health data, and comments written in the school file.
   c. specifying time, date, location, purpose, and length of conference.
   *d. list negative aspects of the student's performance and behavior to convince parents to become more involved in disciplinary practices.
3. According to "Practical Suggestions for Planning and Conducting Parent Conferences," when a teacher uses a written communication to parents as a substitute for, or follow-up to, a conference, this communication should not be:
   a. xeroxed and kept on file.
   *b. negative or emotional in nature.
   c. shown to other colleagues or the school administrator.
   d. written in concise, clear English.

True/False Questions

4. The authors of "Practical Suggestions for Planning and Conducting Parent Conferences" claim that the arrangement of parents and teacher on opposite sides of a table for a conference can inhibit communication. (T)
5. Due process hearings, according to "Practical Suggestions for Planning and Conducting Parent Conferences," that are held in connection with services provided for handicapped students are increasing in frequency. (T)

GENERAL QUESTIONS

6. The authors of "Practical Suggestions for Planning and Conducting Parent Conferences" stated that teachers often have difficulty ending parent conferences. What are some ways in which this difficulty can be overcome?
(set a time limit before meeting begins; discuss agenda items only; avoid overdiscussion of issues; summarize progress periodically; watch for signs of restlessness; make plans for follow-up or additional conference)
7. According to "Practical Suggestions for Planning and Conducting Parent Conferences," why do teachers feel so anxious about conducting parent conferences with parents of handicapped students?
(fear of negative feedback from parents; feelings of blame or guilt for child's lack of achievement; fear that conference will not achieve anything; fear that parents will not attend; fear of inability to communicate; fear that parents may initiate legal action/due process hearing in connection with services not provided their child)
8. Many schools allow students to participate in parent-teacher conferences. According to "Practical Suggestions for Planning and Conducting Parent Conferences," what are some of the pros and cons of this practice?
*(*pro: *student knows what she/he would like to accomplish in next year; increases student's self-esteem to be included; student can mediate misinterpretations of parents and teacher;* con: *both parents and teacher may be uncomfortable discussing student when she/he is present; it may not be feasible to make all the educational changes that student requests at meeting)*

7. WHY NOT ASSUME THEY'RE ALL GIFTED RATHER THAN HANDICAPPED?
RICHARD SALZER
AE p. 36

ARTICLE SUMMARY

This is a scholarly article concerned with the effects of overtesting and overdiagnosing deficits in young children's cognitive development at the beginning of their educational experience. The author contends that testing too early to do specific skills teaching results in two problems: wrong things are done and right ones are not.

KEY TERMS AND TOPICS

Skills Teaching one isolated ability is mastered at a time before the skills are combined into a unified learning process or experience.
Deficit Model program that emphasizes what is wrong in order to correct it.
Standardized Tests tests which have been given to large numbers of randomly selected subjects during development for purposes of comparisons, validity and reliability checks and computations of age norms.

CRITICAL ANALYSIS
Multiple Choice Questions

1. The author of "Why Not Assume They're All Gifted Rather Than Handicapped?" uses the word holistic as most synonymous with which model of education?
   a. skill mastery model.

b. handicapped model.
*c. gifted model.
d. deficit model.

2. Which of the following programs mentioned in "Why Not Assume They're All Gifted Rather Than Handicapped?" is an example of the deficit model in practice?
*a. kindergarten screening to identify at-risk children.
b. Dewey's learning through doing schools.
c. music and story dramatizations in school.
d. programs developed for gifted students.

3. The author of "Why Not Assume They're All Gifted Rather Than Handicapped?" presented a sidebar on Pre-First Grade Literacy Development. Which answer represents his feelings about the material in this sidebar?
a. strongly opposed to it.
*b. strongly supportive of it.
c. amused by it; hopes to amuse readers as well.
d. skeptical of it; asks "Can this work?"

True/False Questions

4. The author of "Why Not Assume They're All Gifted Rather Than Handicapped?" feels the deficit model has credibility with many parents, teachers, and educators because of its connation with technology and medicine. (T)

5. Testing may not be a useful guide to teaching nor a good means of selecting young children for specific programs since young children do not respond reliably to test items, according to "Why Not Assume They're All Gifted Rather Than Handicapped?" (T)

GENERAL QUESTIONS

6. The author of "Why Not Assume They're All Gifted Rather Than Handicapped?" believes that early educational experiences appropriate for gifted students might be more appropriate for handicapped students as well. What are some of these activities which he favors?
(free play, painting, block building, story dramatization, self-expression)

7. According to "Why Not Assume They're All Gifted Rather Than Handicapped?" why have so many adults adopted the attitude that one must find out what is wrong with a child's learning and fix it by teaching them what they do not know?
(desire for higher scores on standardized tests; requests to evaluate programs and demonstrate that instructional objectives are being achieved; societal emphasis on diagnosis and prescription procedures)

8. If society's attitude changes from a deficit model to a gifted model, what might be the pros and cons of this change on special education for handicapped children, according to "Why Not Assume They're All Gifted Rather Than Handicapped?"
*(**pro:** more opportunity to learn and grow in a supportive environment; integration with non-handicapped peers; **con:** specific skills which the exceptional child needs to be taught may be postponed too long; diagnosis and prescription procedures for the actual handicap may be delayed)*

8. CHANGING ATTITUDES,
JOAN KILBURN   AE p. 39

ARTICLE SUMMARY

This article describes a program presented in approximately 225 classrooms in California which was designed to deal with attitudes toward handicapped people on the part of the nonhandicapped. A variety of simulations, discussions, and other activities were led by teams of disabled and nondisabled instructors. The students' responses during the program and afterwards are detailed.

KEY TERMS AND TOPICS

Simulation Stations centers created in the classroom in which students could experience aspects of certain handicaps.
Adventure Game a classroom activity in which the group is given the problem of how to get its members, half of whom are

disabled (blindfolded, in wheelchairs, or on crutches) across an imaginary chasm.

CRITICAL ANALYSIS
Multiple Choice Questions

1. The two meetings of elementary school students with the disabled and the nondisabled instructors in the California program described in "Changing Attitudes" included all of the following curriculum components *except:*
a. simulation stations.
b. sharing of personal experiences.
*c. "What if..." exercises.
d. adventure games.

2. In the article "Changing Attitudes," which of the following is stressed for modifying classroom attitudes about the disabled?
a. providing expert medical knowledge about disabilities.
b. providing special training for teachers.
*c. having people who are disabled act as their own advocates.
d. skillful use of audio-visual materials.

3. In order to maintain contact with schools that have participated in the "Better Understanding" program, what is done every month, according to "Changing Attitudes"?
a. a "Better Understanding" instructor gives a follow-up seminar.
*b. a newsletter "Aware-News" is sent to participating classrooms.
c. students take a field trip to a facility serving handicapped persons.
d. teachers attend a workshop to learn how to do related "Better Understanding" activities in their classrooms.

True/False Questions

4. According to "Changing Attitudes," the ultimate goal of the "Better Understanding" program is to adapt the environment so that each student or adult, whether disabled or not, can participate actively and with satisfaction. (T)

5. Some elementary school children became more frightened of disabled persons after participating in the "Better Understanding" program, according to "Changing Attitudes." (F)

GENERAL QUESTIONS

6. The author of "Changing Attitudes" argues that the program it describes has had a significant impact upon student attitudes toward disabilities. What evidence does it cite and do you find it convincing?
(the evidence is from written and oral comments of students before and after sessions; convincing evidence should be related to validity of verbal vs. behavioral measures of change and to whether or not a more controlled testing is required)

7. The author of "Changing Attitudes" argues that the attitudes of the nonhandicapped population toward persons with disabilities play a deciding role in the ultimate success or failure of endeavors to integrate handicapped persons more fully into society. How would you evaluate the relative importance of the attitudes and behaviors of the handicapped vs. those of the nonhandicapped in affecting such integration?
(factors to consider include: extent to which nonhandicapped determine opportunity; political and social power developed by the handicapped themselves; importance of acceptance of discrimination and low expectations by the handicapped themselves; and effect of the attitudes of each group upon the other)

8. In "Changing Attitudes," what is the role of programs designed to affect the attitudes of nonhandicapped students within the overall process of mainstreaming?
(the psychological importance of acceptance of handicapped by nonhandicapped students; the knowledge of how to interact with handicapped as a basis for mutual aid with educational and social tasks in the classroom; the need to prevent harassment and insulting of handicapped students in order to maintain a good educational environment)

9. PROMOTING HANDICAP AWARENESS IN PRESCHOOL CHILDREN,
DALE BAUM AND CAROL WELLS   AE p. 43

ARTICLE SUMMARY

In the first part of this paper, the authors review research on how and when children develop awarenss of differences in people. They suggest that the preschool and primary years are the best time to teach children positive attitudes toward handicapped persons. The remainder of the paper suggests activities which can be used to help children learn these positive attitudes.

KEY TERMS AND TOPICS

Mainstreaming educating handicapped and nonhandicapped students in regular classroom settings.
Preschool Programs programs which provide opportunities for young children to explore and manipulate materials and share activities with other young children before formal education begins.
Dramatic Play make-believe play where children pretend to be other people and use materials in imaginative ways to represent other objects or situations.

CRITICAL ANALYSIS
Multiple Choice Questions

1. According to research reported in "Promoting Handicap Awareness in Preschool Children," children's awareness of handicapping conditions at age 4 is followed by ___ at about age 5.
   *a. negativism
   b. positivism
   c. correct labeling
   d. compassion and empathy
2. Samples of learning activities which can be used to promote handicap awareness are suggested in "Promoting Handicap Awareness in Preschool Children" for all of the following preschool subjects *except:*
   a. snack time.
   b. language.
   c. science.
   *d. math.
3. In "Promoting Handicap Awareness in Preschool Children," suggestions for fostering handicap awareness through dramatic play focused on the handicapping conditions of:
   a. deafness and speech impairments.
   *b. blindness and orthopedic impairments.
   c. mental retardation and learning disabilities.
   d. emotional disturbances and health impairments.

True/False Questions

4. "Promoting Handicap Awareness in Preschool Children" says that children are least accepting of human differences during their preschool and early primary years. (F)
5. Research reported in "Promoting Handicap Awareness in Preschool Children" suggests that as children grow older more positive attitudes naturally replace the negative attitudes expressed toward handicapped persons at earlier age levels. (F)

GENERAL QUESTIONS

6. The authors of "Promoting Handicap Awareness in Preschool Children" suggested many activities to help young children learn about handicaps. Give one awareness activity which can be used to teach about each of the major areas of handicapping conditions.
   (LD: story, film; MR: story, film; speech: science, dramatic play; ED: story, film; hearing: language, science; vision: dramatic play, science; orthopedic: art, dramatic play; other health problems: science, snack time)
7. The article "Promoting Handicap Awareness in Preschool Children," states that "The relatively small effort required to implement such a program has the potential for an enormous

return for both handicapped and nonhandicapped children." What are some of the returns for handicapped children? For nonhandicapped children?
   (handicapped: greater acceptance, higher self-esteem, integration into society, more emphasis on ability over disability; nonhandicapped: less prejudice, higher self-esteem, more compassion, more ability to empathize)
8. After reading "Promoting Handicap Awareness in Preschool Children," why do you think it is easier to change attitudes toward handicapped persons in the preschool and primary years than later?
   (more accepting of differences; less prejudicial; fewer experiences with handicapped persons to color judgments; more willing to accept adults' judgments; readily model behavior of significant others)

10. MODIFYING THE ATTITUDES OF NONHANDICAPPED HIGH SCHOOL STUDENTS TOWARD HANDICAPPED PEERS,
CRAIG R. FIEDLER AND RICHARD L. SIMPSON
          AE p. 48

ARTICLE SUMMARY

This is a research article comparing two programs designed to positively modify the attitudes of nonhandicapped high school students toward their handicapped peers. A curriculum structured around categories of exceptionality produced greater attitude change than a noncategorical curriculum. Both curricula produced more attitude change than occurred in a control group.

KEY TERMS AND TOPICS

Labeling applying a name to a condition which may have the effect of causing both the labelers and the labeled persons to see the condition as unidimensional rather than appreciating the uniqueness of each person so labeled.
Categorical Curriculum a course of study of handicapping conditions structured around information about each labeled category of disability (e.g., LD, MR, ED).
Noncategorical Curriculum a course of study of handicapping conditions structured around social, ecological, and psychological issues related to disabled persons without labeling their specific condition.

CRITICAL ANALYSIS
Multiple Choice Questions

1. According to the discussion of normalization in "Modifying the Attitudes of Nonhandicapped High School Students Toward Handicapped Peers," this normalization principle stresses service in environments that are:
   a. as physically and emotionally therapeutic as possible.
   b. unaffected by any persons with any handicapping conditions.
   c. prepared to provide as much compensatory education as possible.
   *d. as culturally normal as possible.
2. The authors of "Modifying the Attitudes of Nonhandicapped High School Students Toward Handicapped Peers" contend that a label designating a handicapping condition may create a barrier to understanding a uniquely handicapped individual for all of the following reasons *except* that the labeled person is:
   *a. segregated from all other persons because of the label.
   b. perceived as being like all other persons with that label.
   c. treated like all other persons with that label.
   d. apt to use the label as an excuse for not achieving up to his or her capabilities.
3. One area of exceptionality was not discussed in the categorical curriculum in "Modifying the Attitudes of Nonhandicapped High School Students Toward Handicapped Peers," probably because the prevalence of this disability is low in the high school population. This category is:
   a. emotionally disabled.
   b. learning disabled.

because the prevalence of this disability is low in the high school population. This category is:
a. emotionally disabled.
b. learning disabled.
*c. speech impaired.
d. health impaired.

True/False Questions

4. According to "Modifying the Attitudes of Nonhandicapped High School Students Toward Handicapped Peers," males held significantly more favorable attitudes toward handicapped persons than their female counterparts. (F)
5. "Modifying the Attitudes of Nonhandicapped High School Students Toward Handicapped Peers" states that, in some cases, labeling by handicap may increase peer acceptance of a handicapped child by making his or her behavior more acceptable. (T)

GENERAL QUESTIONS

6. Describe some of the lessons which were taught in the noncategorical curriculum described in "Modifying the Attitudes of Nonhandicapped High School Students Toward Handicapped Peers."
(effects of labels; individual differences; values; handicapping dependencies; self-fulfilling prophecies of dependency; normalization; short-term solutions; self-advocacy; benefits of integration of disabled people)
7. The authors of "Modifying the Attitudes of Nonhandicapped High School Students Toward Handicapped Peers" quoted Martin as warning that unless educators develop strategies for creating an acceptance by students in regular education for their handicapped peers, "...we will subject many children to a painful and frustrating educational experience in the name of progress." What progress was he talking about? What children? And why?
(progress: mainstreaming; children: handicapped students; why: they will be judged by label rather than by individuality; they will be rejected, ridiculed, kept dependent; self-fulfilling prophecy may be operative)
8. Educators are always looking for better ways to reach attitude change. According to "Modifying the Attitudes of Nonhandicapped High School Students Toward Handicapped Peers," why can a categorical curriculum succeed even though labeling is known to have some detrimental effects? Why can a noncategorical curriculum make students uncomfortable?
(pro/categories: fill cognitive void about categories; replace stereotypes and misinformation about categories with fact; con/noncategorical curriculum: putting students' personal beliefs and values under scrutiny creates discomfort; asking students to assume some responsibility for improving life conditions of handicapped creates discomfort)

11. A SUCCESSFUL HANDICAP AWARENESS PROGRAM—RUN BY SPECIAL PARENTS,
BETTY BINKARD   AE p. 55

ARTICLE SUMMARY

This is a general interest article which describes a Minnesota group's successful program to involve parents of handicapped children in advocacy programs, and to build positive attitudes toward handicapped persons through the efforts of the parent advocates.

KEY TERMS AND TOPICS

Advocacy Groups persons united together to champion, defend, espouse, and plead in favor of more public support for some particular cause.
PACER a Minnesota-based coalition of advocacy groups for the handicapped who obtained funding to help teach their state's parents about PL 94-142 and train them to work effectively with schools.
CMI (Count Me In) a handicap awareness program designed by parents and presented in schools by parents.

CRITICAL ANALYSIS

Multiple Choice Questions

1. As told in "A Successful Handicap Awareness Program," what vehicle did parents use in their school presentations to increase positive attitudes toward children with handicaps?
a. showed filmstrips about handicapped children.
*b. put on puppet shows about handicapped children.
c. read stories about handicapped children.
d. held classroom discussions on handicapping conditions.
2. The CMI program described in "A Successful Handicap Awareness Program" was first developed for use in:
*a. preschools and primary schools.
b. secondary schools.
c. meetings of members of the business community.
d. meetings of recreational, health, and medical professionals.
3. As described in "A Successful Handicap Awareness Program," the scripts used in CMI presentations were developed to deal with all of the following *except:*
a. sports activities.
b. family problems.
c. emotional dilemmas.
*d. religious philosophies.

True/False Questions

4. According to "A Successful Handicap Awareness Program," the CMI program is limited to the State of Minnesota. (F)
5. "A Successful Handicap Awareness Program" states that CMI presentations include the use of both handicapped and nonhandicapped figures. (T)

GENERAL QUESTIONS

6. The CMI presentation described in "A Successful Handicap Awareness Program" was from 45-60 minutes in total length but was broken down into five or six different 7-10 minute scripts dealing with different disabilities and different dilemmas. What are the advantages of thus giving several lessons in one presentation?
(hold viewer's attention; present information about more types of disabilities; present disabled as experiencing many real life situations similar to nondisabled persons' situations; provide opportunity for more parents to be involved in each presentation)
7. What benefits could accrue from presentations of the CMI program described in "A Successful Handicap Awareness Program" to groups such as businessmen and women, health professionals, recreational program directors, and other interested adults?
(help change attitudes of adults in more positive directions; help adults who serve as role models how to interact with the handicapped; enlist support of adults for continuing such programs in schools; solicit funds from adults to help support such school programs)
8. What are several ways in which regular classroom teachers can continue to promote handicap awareness and acceptance after a structured program such as the CMI presentation, as shown in "A Successful Handicap Awareness Program"?
(present information on other disabilities in class; lead discussions on interactions with handicapped persons; read or provide books to be read about handicapped persons; show films about persons with handicaps; invite handicapped persons to speak to their classes)

12. HOW DO WE HELP THE LEARNING DISABLED?
JUDITH DOLGINS, MARCEE MYERS, PATRICIA A. FLYNN, AND JOSSIE MOORE   AE p. 62

ARTICLE SUMMARY

This article for general education teachers discusses the nature of learning disability, the various ways it is manifested, and strategies for teaching learning disabled children. The article presents suggestions for parents of learning disabled children.

KEY TERMS AND TOPICS

Learning Disability discrepancy in learning in one or more areas up to one's ability level which is not clearly related to mental retardation, brain damage, emotional disorder, environmental deprivation, poor vision or hearing, or lack of motivation.

Closure definition of a sequence as parts of a whole which permits analysis or synthesis of the whole.

CRITICAL ANALYSIS
Multiple Choice Questions

1. As stated in "How Do We Help the Learning Disabled?" a widely used definition of a learning disability is an exclusion definition. It excludes children with all of the following from an LD classification *except* those with:
    a. environmental deprivation.
    *b. variability in task performance.
    c. emotional disturbance.
    d. mental retardation.
2. LD children who have difficulties remembering the sequence of things heard such as telephone numbers, directions, and oral questions are described in "How Do We Help the Learning Disabled?" as having:
    *a. auditory channel deficits.
    b. weak visual skills.
    c. short attention spans.
    d. auditory discrimination problems.
3. Parents of LD children can modify the home situation to help their LD children function more successfully. All of the following were presented as pointers for parents in "How Do We Help the Learning Disabled?" *except:*
    a. providing a quiet place where the LD child can work.
    b. being consistent with discipline.
    *c. having learning sessions last 40 minutes or longer.
    d. demonstrating tasks as well as explaining them.

True/False Questions

4. According to "How Do We Help the Learning Disabled?" frequent reinforcements enhance the learning process in LD children. (T)
5. Researchers still do not understand the causes of LD nor do they know how to cure them, according to "How Do We Help the Learning Disabled?" (T)

GENERAL QUESTIONS

6. What are some of the areas in which learning disabled children are likely to have deficits, according to "How Do We Help the Learning Disabled?"
    (visual skills; auditory channel deficits; auditory processing skills; integrating visual and auditory skills; visual figure-ground perception; auditory figure-ground perception; closure, memory, and language disorders)
7. What are some of the forms of emotional support teachers are encouraged to give learning disabled students in "How Do We Help the Learning Disabled?"
    (support for self-esteem by keeping folders demonstrating student progress and indicating that everyone has problems; frequent reinforcement through verbal and nonverbal signs)
8. "How Do We Help the Learning Disabled?" describes a teacher who uses the students' desire to put on a play as a way of motivating a series of learning activities. Analyze how she did so.
    (initial desire came from students who wanted to put on play; choice of play students would identify with; frustration of desire by withdrawing scripts; channeling into vocabulary lessons; demand to prove comprehension of script; support for memorization of script through appropriate cueing; mobilization of artistic skills for costumes and backdrop; performance to other students and teachers and recognition for its quality)

13. THE LEARNING DISABLED PRESCHOOL CHILD,
SAMUEL A. KIRK   AE p. 68

ARTICLE SUMMARY

In this scholarly article, the author differentiates between developmental and academic learning disabilities. He believes developmental learning disabilities can and should be assessed in the preschool years and that early intervention can help ameliorate later problems.

KEY TERMS AND TOPICS

Learning Disability discrepancy in learning in one or more areas up to one's ability level which is not clearly related to brain damage, emotional disorder, deprivation, retardation, or lack of motivation.

Developmental Learning Disability LD which affects a prerequisite skill needed for learning such as a disorder in attention, in visual or auditory perception, in memory, in thinking, or in language.

Academic Learning Disability a deficit in reading, writing, spelling, written expression, or calculation at the school-age level.

CRITICAL ANALYSIS
Multiple Choice Questions

1. According to "The Learning Disabled Preschool Child," all of the following are developmental learning disabilities *except:*
    a. memory disorder.
    b. attention disorder.
    c. thinking disorder.
    *d. reading disorder.
2. According to the author of "The Learning Disabled Preschool Child," a writing disorder can be identified:
    a. in infancy.
    b. at the preschool-age level.
    *c. at the school-age level.
    d. in adolescence.
3. Ability profiles of two children were illustrated in Figure 1 in "The Learning Disabled Preschool Child." The child whose graph showed very few discrepancies among abilities and a relatively even profile from age 2 through 6 was described as having:
    *a. mental retardation.
    b. a developmental learning disability.
    c. an academic learning disability.
    d. normal learning ability.

True/False Questions

4. According to "The Learning Disabled Preschool Child," many developmental disabilities, although initially caused by a biological problem, are prolonged or exacerbated by the environment. (T)
5. The authors of "The Learning Disabled Preschool Child" state that intensive early intervention cannot ameliorate developmental disabilities which are the result of a neurologist deficit. (F)

GENERAL QUESTIONS

6. According to the author of "The Learning Disabled Preschool Child," a biological defect at an early age may set in motion a pattern of behaviors by child and parents which perpetuate the defect and create disabilities in learning. What are some of these child behaviors and parent behaviors?
    (child: avoids activities which are not rewarding; withdraws from activities related to defect; compensates by overengaging in activities which are rewarding; gives excuses for not attempting difficult activities; parents: avoid asking child to do

things from which child naturally withdraws; ask child to show off in activities which child can accomplish)

7. According to "The Learning Disabled Preschool Child," should all children be assessed for developmental learning disabilities in the preschool-age level? What would be the pros and cons of such mass assessment?
(pro: intervention can be started early with the probable result of ameliorating disabilities and preventing academic problems; prevent some later misdiagnosis of mental retardation; con: expensive; many normal children may be mistakenly diagnosed as having a developmental LD due to problems with testing validity and reliability; problems associated with labeling of deficits and self-fulfilling prophecy)

8. Using information from "The Learning Disabled Preschool Child," differentiate between a developmental learning disability and an academic learning disability.
(developmental: deficit(s) in attention, perception, memory, thinking, or language identifiable at pre-school level; academic: deficit(s) in reading, writing, spelling, written expression, or calculation identifiable at school-age level)

14. FACTS ABOUT CHILDHOOD HYPERACTIVITY,
JAMES HADLEY   AE p. 71

ARTICLE SUMMARY

This article is a concise overview of the hyperactive/attention deficit disorder syndrome including information on diagnosis, causes, treatment, controversy over various treatments, psychological concerns and suggestions for dealing with children with the disorder. The author provides a list of sources for more information on the syndrome as well.

KEY TERMS AND TOPICS

Hyperactivity excessive motor activity, short attention span, and impulsive behavior for the child's age in the absence of emotional disorder or mental retardation.
Attentional Deficit Disorder new APA term for hyperactive and hypoactive children who have a diminished ability to attend to the task at hand and who behave impulsively.

CRITICAL ANALYSIS
Multiple Choice Questions

1. Childhood hyperactivity has been in the medical literature for over 100 years and has been called by many names. According to "Facts About Childhood Hyperactivity," the current standard diagnostic label for it put forth by the American Psychiatric Association is:
   a. minimal brain dysfunction.
   b. hyperkinetic syndrome.
   c. minor cerebral dysfunction.
   *d. attention deficit disorder.

2. Which of the following is *not* one of the primary treatments discussed in the article "Facts About Childhood Hyperactivity" for relieving the symptoms of this syndrome?
   a. psychological counseling
   b. diet therapy
   c. stimulant drug therapy
   *d. antipsychotic drug therapy

3. The article, "Facts About Childhood Hyperactivity," presented a list of suggestions for people who deal with hyperactive children. All of the following were mentioned *except:*
   *a. avoid an excessively positive approach such as "good," "go on," "yes."
   b. let the child perform one task at a time.
   c. avoid pity, overindulgence and teasing of the child.
   d. keep your emotions "cool."

True/False Questions

4. According to "Facts About Childhood Hyperactivity," the consensus of several scientific investigations of diet and hyperactivity was that special restricted diets which eliminate artificial food additives and some natural salicylates should be routinely prescribed for hyperactive children. (F)

5. "Facts About Childhood Hyperactivity" states that attention deficit disorder with hyperactivity is much more common in boys than in girls. (T)

GENERAL QUESTIONS

6. Attention deficit disorder with hyperactivity is classified as a syndrome because it has a cluster of symptoms and no known single cause. List several symptoms as described in "Facts About Childhood Hyperactivity" and several suggested causative factors.
(symptoms: excessive motor activity, short attention span, impulsive behavior, poor sleep, distractibility, inappropriate behavior; causes: prematurity, head trauma, infections, lead poisoning, thyroid disease, family discord, dietary factors, vitamin deficiencies)

7. Dr. Benjamin Feingold's diet for hyperactive children has been a controversial subject since it was first tried in 1963. It eliminates foods with salicylates, preservatives, artificial flavors and colors and industrial processing from the child's diet. As stated in "Facts About Childhood Hyperactivity," why do some professionals and parents find this diet objectionable?
(child cannot eat same foods as family, peers; hard to implement this diet in keeping with many ethnic and cultural food preferences; expensive to provide this diet; special time-consuming shopping and cooking is necessary to implement this diet; research studies have not been able to support all the claims made by the Feingold diet)

8. Why does attention deficit disorder with hyperactivity fit more appropriately in the special education classification of learning disability rather than in the classification of either emotional disability or health impairment, according to "Facts About Childhood Hyperactivity"?
(short attention span and distractibility make learning difficult; no clear evidence that emotional factors cause the problem although they do aggravate it; health impairment may follow restless sleep and poor appetite but the attention deficit causes the health problems rather than vice-versa)

15. RECOGNIZING SPECIAL TALENTS IN LEARNING DISABLED STUDENTS,
SUSAN BAUM AND ROBERT KIRSCHENBAUM
AE p. 77

ARTICLE SUMMARY

This scholarly article discusses ways in which learning disabled students can be further assessed to identify their special talents. The authors contend that LD children can also be intellectually gifted. Suggestions are offered for supporting LD students within the school environment.

KEY TERMS AND TOPICS

Gifted Behavior above-average intellectual ability, task commitment, and creativity brought to bear upon a specific area of knowledge.
Enrichment Triad Model a program developed by Renzulli designed to allow gifted children to identify their interests and strengths and pursue them.

CRITICAL ANALYSIS
Multiple Choice Questions

1. According to a study reported in "Recognizing Special Talents in Learning Disabled Students," when highly verbal LD students were placed with their gifted peers in a simulation activity requiring problem solving:
   a. the two groups were in constant conflict.
   *b. the two groups could not be distinguished from each other.
   c. the LD students performed more effectively.
   d. the gifted students developed a tutor role toward the LD students.

2. Figure 1 in "Recognizing Special Talents in Learning Disabled Students" presented indications of special talents in a boy

discussed in the text named "Neil." Which was *not* one of the categories illustrating his strengths?
- a. above average intellectual ability.
- b. task commitment.
- c. creative ability.
- *d. photography.

3. The case study of Neil in the article "Recognizing Special Talents in Learning Disabled Students" revealed that he had produced an essay entitled "How I Feel About School" which was subsequently presented to workshops and conferences throughout the USA and Canada. This essay was completed as:
- a. a written thesis.
- b. a record album.
- *c. a photographic display.
- d. an epic poem.

True/False Questions

4. According to "Recognizing Special Talents in Learning Disabled Students," emotional support is often necessary to help LD students cope with their self-perceptions of inconsistency. (T)

5. It can be profoundly destructive to a student's self-esteem to be labeled and treated only in terms of a learning disability, according to "Recognizing Special Talents in Learning Disabled Students." (T)

GENERAL QUESTIONS

6. What criticisms of the school's approach are implied in the way the school treated "Neil" in "Recognizing Special Talents in Learning Disabled Students"?
(focused on weaknesses; failed to recognize creativity; used strengths to focus on weaknesses; did not recognize his need to define his own tasks)

7. How does "Recognizing Special Talents in Learning Disabled Students" suggest that children be screened for their areas of giftedness?
(gather information from outside as well as inside school setting; look for above-average abilities; look for task commitment; look for creativity)

8. According to "Recognizing Special Talents in Learning Disabled Students," what are the elements of the Enrichment Triad Model proposed for discovering and encouraging learning disabled students in their areas of gifted behavior?
(no-fail exploratory activities to identify areas of interest; enrichment activities focused on higher-level thinking activities such as critical thinking, creativity and problem-solving; student investigation of real problems)

16. TEAM TEACHING THE LEARNING DISABLED CHILD,
MARY B. DENAULT   AE p. 81

ARTICLE SUMMARY

This is a general interest, personal experience account of how a teacher assigned to a special class for LD students stumbled upon the concept of team teaching. The author contends that shared teaching efforts use time more efficiently, reduce discipline problems, and allow for more individual attention to students.

KEY TERMS AND TOPICS

Team Teaching two or more teachers share one class, plan lessons together, and divide responsibilities so that some students will have individual attention while others are having group lessons.
Integrated Curriculum using one lesson or project to teach two or more subjects simultaneously.

CRITICAL ANALYSIS

Multiple Choice Questions

1. In the article "Team Teaching the Learning Disabled Child," a lesson on restaurants was expanded to integrate several subjects into one curriculum unit. Which school subject was not a part of this integrated curriculum?
- *a. physical education.
- b. social studies.
- c. math.
- d. English.

2. The LD students described in "Team Teaching the Learning Disabled Child" were in which type of learning environment?
- a. regular classroom.
- b. resource room.
- *c. special class.
- d. residential institution.

3. Which was not a benefit of team teaching described by the author of "Team Teaching the Learning Disabled Child"?
- *a. dramatic increments on achievement test scores.
- b. reduced discipline problems.
- c. more efficient use of time.
- d. good preparation for mainstreaming.

True/False Questions

4. "Team Teaching the Learning Disabled Child" states that a disadvantage of team teaching is that students whose classes are made larger by combining with other classes suffer a consequent loss of self-esteem. (F)

5. Integrating several subjects into one curriculum is confusing to learning disabled students, according to "Team Teaching the Learning Disabled Child." (F)

GENERAL QUESTIONS

6. The author of "Team Teaching the Learning Disabled Child" described a meaningful and practical lesson on restaurants for 30 LD students. What were some of the tasks she assigned these students in this lesson?
(write up menus; compose ads; price menus; figure tips; figure taxes; tabulate customers' bills; serve as cooks; serve as waiters; write customers' orders; clean up)

7. What evidence did the author of "Team Teaching the Learning Disabled Child" give to support the idea that combining classes and team teaching is good for students? What types of problems might arise from this type of educational programming?
(support: *students felt less "different" in larger class; more efficient use of time; time for individual attention to students in need; fewer discipline problems;* **potential problems:** *competition or jealousy between team teachers; protocol considerations with such large classes; desire to keep students in special classes to maintain need for team rather than to mainstream them; budget considerations of paying two teachers to teach one class)*

8. PL 94-142 mandates that children be taught in the least restrictive environment compatible with their handicap. According to "Team Teaching the Learning Disabled Child," what arguments can be offered (pro and con) for a segregated, special, team-taught class being less restrictive (pro) and more restrictive (con) for LD students?
(pro: *larger "special" team-taught class makes each LD student feel less different than others and approximates a mainstreamed regular classroom while offering more special services for learning disabled students;* **con:** *LD child is not learning to interact with non-LD students when kept in special class for full school day)*

17. AN EXPERIENCE IN FRUSTRATION: SIMULATIONS APPROXIMATING LEARNING DIFFICULTIES,
DONNA RASCHKE AND CHARLES DEDRICK

AE p. 83

ARTICLE SUMMARY

This article describes a special program in which non-learning disabled persons are sensitized to the feelings that accompany the inability to process educational materials. The authors contend that this type of experience and subsequent understanding will enhance future interactions between LD students and their non-LD peers.

KEY TERMS AND TOPICS

Simulation Activities activities which assume the appearance of something that they, in reality, are not.

CRITICAL ANALYSIS

Multiple Choice Questions

1. Many simulation activities designed to help sensitize nonhandicapped persons to handicapped persons' feelings have been developed. Which new simulation activity is described in the article "An Experience in Frustration"?
   a. one approximating a visual impairment.
   b. one emphasizing an orthopedic handicap.
   c. one approximating a hearing impairment.
   *d. one emphasizing auditory processing skills.
2. The two new simulation activities described in "An Experience in Frustration" focus on more understanding of ___ in learning processes.
   a. mathematical paradigms
   *b. individual differences
   c. visual responsiveness
   d. auditory discrimination
3. The simulation activity leader described in "An Experience in Frustration" attempted to elicit all of the following responses from the followers *except:*
   a. confusion.
   b. frustration.
   c. anxiety.
   *d. disobedience.

True/False Questions

4. In "An Experience in Frustration," the simulation activity called "Around the World" is used to sensitize persons to a learning disability with mental mathematical computations. (T)
5. According to "An Experience in Frustration," educational simulation activities, in general, promote attitudinal change and a greater respect for the learning differences which exist among people. (T)

GENERAL QUESTIONS

6. The simulation activity called "Simon Says" had several modifications in "An Experience in Frustration," from the standard "Simon Says" game designed to help participants appreciate the difficulties which some LD persons have following spoken directions. What directions did participants have to remember and follow?
   (only react when direction is preceded by "Simon Says"; reverse the directions of right and left on feet only; reverse the directions of over and under)
7. The simulation leader described in "An Experience in Frustration" intentionally patronized the participants, insulted them, ridiculed them, and selected out some individuals for special criticism. What makes this an effective teaching style? Under what circumstances could this teaching style be detrimental?
   (effective: anxiety is first heightened and then relieved in group discussion; participants feel grateful to leader for relieving their anxiety as well as more empathetic to students who feel this

way six hours/day, 180 days/year without the possibility of relief; detrimental: some participants may continue to harbor resentment toward the leader for creating so much frustration and humiliation; some participants may be LD, or may believe they are LD, and may not obtain any relief through group discussion following simulation activities)
8. The simulation activities described in "An Experience in Frustration" were conducted with elementary school children. In what other groups could they effectively be used?
   (college classrooms; high schools; teachers' seminars; parent meetings; paraprofessional/staff in-service training sessions; special classes)

18. CHANGES IN MILD MENTAL RETARDATION: POPULATION, PROGRAMS, AND PERSPECTIVES,
EDWARD A. POLLOWAY AND J. DAVID SMITH

AE p. 90

ARTICLE SUMMARY

The definition of educable mental retardation has changed in recent years, as have the characteristics of those so labeled. This article surveys the causes of that change and discusses its implications for educational programming.

KEY TERMS AND TOPICS

EMR educable mental retardation and mild retardation. Adaptive students likely to demonstrate the skills associated with a success in mainstream programs and post-school adjustment.
SOMPA System of Multicultural Pluralistic Assessment developed by Mercer and Lewis to provide culturally unbiased assessment of retardation.

CRITICAL ANALYSIS

Multiple Choice Questions

1. The authors of "Changes in Mild Mental Retardation" give all of the following as reasons for the decreased interest in mild (educable) mentally retarded persons *except:*
   *a. raising of the ceiling IQ score for EMR placement from 70 to 85.
   b. the formulation of learning disabilities as a separate category.
   c. the formulation of severe or multi-handicapped, as a separate category.
   d. a change in the population served under the mild EMR label.
2. "Changes in Mild Mental Retardation" states that the System of Multicultural Pluralistic Assessment (SOMPA) offers a method for the adjustment of IQ scores based on:
   a. degree of chronicity.
   *b. sociocultural status.
   c. biological parents' IQ scores.
   d. number of other concurrent handicapping conditions.
3. According to research cited in "Changes in Mild Mental Retardation," students classified as EMR are more likely than students in the general school population to have all of the following *except:*
   a. inadequate nutritional and health care provisions.
   b. restricted oral language skills.
   *c. parents who overemphasize educational achievement.
   d. male chromosomal configuration.

True/False Questions

4. According to "Changes in Mild Mental Retardation," today Down's syndrome children are more frequently classified as "educable" than they were in the past. (T)
5. "Changes in Mild Mental Retardation" states that litigation has resulted in more minority children being classified as EMR in recent years. (F)

6. What factors are suggested in the article "Changes in Mild Mental Retardation" to explain the drop in children in retardation programs from 1976-77 to 1980-81 in most states?
   (use of adaptive behavior as well as IQ criteria; changing of IQ ceiling; effort to eliminate culture-determined effects)
7. According to "Changes in Mild Mental Retardation," what changes in the characteristics of EMR children have probably been occurring over the past decade?
   (less a cultural-familial designation, more determined by specific pathological causes; reduced experience of defeat and frustration in school due to EMR or preschool programs for the handicapped and early referral; fear behavior disorders due to growth of programs for disturbed or disordered children; increased gap between chronological ages and achievement level in school due to increasing severity of handicap in EMR category; increased language delay; lower intellectual level)
8. What danger does the article "Changes in Mild Mental Retardation" see in the current trend toward mainstreaming of EMR children? Do you agree?
   (inappropriate emphasis on academic rather than vocational and life adaptation capacities)

19. THE CHILD WITH DOWN'S SYNDROME,
MERRIL HARRIS   AE p. 99

ARTICLE SUMMARY

This article is written expressly for those who work in early education programs which are taking mentally retarded children. It discusses the causes, symptoms, and characteristics of Down's syndrome and suggests how teachers should relate to Down's children and integrate them into a normal preschool early education program.

KEY TERMS AND TOPICS

Down's Syndrome a condition caused by chromosomal abnormality which causes a wide range of physical abnormalities as well as mental retardation.

CRITICAL ANALYSIS

Multiple Choice Questions

1. According to "The Child With Down's Syndrome," what is the area of least development in a Down's syndrome child?
   a. weight and head circumference.
   b. muscular coordination.
   *c. speech and language.
   d. pigmentation of eyes, skin and hair.
2. The author of "The Child With Down's Syndrome" urges that Down's syndrome children be given more than the usual amount of:
   a. foods containing the ten essential amino acids.
   *b. sensory stimulation.
   c. sexual stimulation.
   d. protection from viruses and bacteria.
3. According to "The Child With Down's Syndrome," physical characteristics of Down's syndrome persons include all of the following except:
   a. flattened nasal bridge.
   *b. muscle spasticity.
   c. protruding tongue.
   d. short arms and legs.

True/False Questions

4. According to "The Child With Down's Syndrome," Down's syndrome is characterized by an absence of a portion of genetic material on the 21st chromosome. (F)
5. "The Child With Down's Syndrome" states that Down's syndrome is now known to be caused by an autoimmune disease which afflicts many older mothers. (F)

6. What does the author of "The Child With Down's Syndrome" recommend that teachers do to compensate for the poor verbal capacities of Down's syndrome children?
   (make instructions simple, well-structured, and clearly spoken; combine with gestures; pantomime an activity; manipulate student through proper motions or actions; break down skills and activities)
7. What are some of the fallacious opinions regarding children with Down's syndrome that "The Child With Down's Syndrome" attempts to dispel?
   (that Down's children can't learn to walk, talk, toilet train, feed and dress themselves; read, write, count, socialize, understand verbal communication, complete formal education through or even beyond high school; enjoy socializing as young adults, and live independently as contributing members of society)
8. Why does the author of "The Child With Down's Syndrome" urge that children with Down's syndrome be treated no differently from other children except for more active stimulation, and more detailed direction?
   (children may try to test adult in charge, children may take advantage of label "poor mentally retarded child")

20. USING TASK VARIATION TO MOTIVATE HANDICAPPED STUDENTS,
LEE KERN DUNLAP   AE p. 101

ARTICLE SUMMARY

This is a general interest article for teachers describing a task variation approach to education. The authors contend that this approach increases the motivation and the learning rate of students with mental retardation and many other types of handicaps as well.

KEY TERMS AND TOPICS

Task Variation selection and scheduling of tasks within a teaching lesson so that the student is presented with both mastered and unmastered tasks intermittently.

CRITICAL ANALYSIS

Multiple Choice Questions

1. According to the author of "Using Task Variation to Motivate Handicapped Students," the task variation approach is the opposite of which other commonly used educational approach?
   a. open education approach.
   *b. constant task approach.
   c. Montessori approach.
   d. discovery learning approach.
2. In the article "Using Task Variation to Motivate Handicapped Students," examples were given of how to use the task variation approach of teaching in all of the following situations except:
   *a. large group discussion.
   b. small group instruction.
   c. individual instruction.
   d. one-to-one interaction outside the classroom.
3. The authors of "Using Task Variation to Motivate Handicapped Students" suggested all of the following benefits of using this approach except:
   a. reduce off-task behaviors.
   b. increase enthusiasm for instructional activity.
   c. increase rate of learning.
   *d. reduce need for reinforcement procedures.

True/False Questions

4. According to "Using Task Variation to Motivate Handicapped Students," constant task strategies often result in declining

levels of motivation and performance and increase in off-task behaviors. (T)

5. "Using Task Variation to Motivate Handicapped Students" states that for relatively difficult tasks, constant task sequences produce more rapid and more efficient learning than task variation procedures. (F)

GENERAL QUESTIONS

6. The author of "Using Task Variation to Motivate Handicapped Students" suggests that the optimal number of new tasks to be presented during a session depends on the task and the student. What task characteristics would reduce the number of tasks to be presented? What student characteristics would reduce the number of tasks to be presented?
(task: difficulty, length of time needed for presentation, length of time needed for response, type of task, e.g., verbal, written, demonstration; student: motivation, cognitive ability, persistence, distractibility, emotional status)

7. Traditionally, teachers have used a constant task (or massed trials) approach for teaching new tasks. According to "Using Task Variation to Motivate Handicapped Students," what are some arguments that a teacher who has always used the constant task approach might offer as reasons for not changing to the task variation approach?
(waste time reviewing tasks the child has mastered; confuse child about what new task is when continually asked about old task; increase length of time child will need to learn new task; not a good method for use in teaching the entire class a new task)

8. The authors of "Using Task Variation to Motivate Handicapped Students" relate the task variation approach to teaching children who are mentally retarded or learning disabled. What other types of students could benefit from this educational procedure?
(gifted; visually impaired; hearing impaired; speech impaired; emotionally disturbed; orthopedically impaired; other health impaired; multihandicapped; normal learner)

21. LEARNING THROUGH OUTDOOR ADVENTURE EDUCATION,
ROGER D. FRANT, CHRISTOPHER C. ROLAND, AND PAUL SCHEMPP   AE p. 105

ARTICLE SUMMARY

The article describes a program for moderately to severely mentally retarded people from nine to 56 years old held at a wilderness camp. Adventure activities such as new games, initiative/problem-solving tasks, and rope courses were used for a variety of emotional and social objectives. Results are evaluated and application to normal school environments discussed.

KEY TERMS AND TOPICS

New Games an alternative to traditionally competitive games; in new games no one is eliminated and everybody wins.
Initiative/Problem-Solving Tasks problems posed to small groups to solve by using physical objects ingeniously.
Debriefing a discussion, immediately after an activity, designed for group reflection on the results.

CRITICAL ANALYSIS
Multiple Choice Questions

1. One of the goals of the camping program described in "Learning Through Outdoor Adventure Education" was:
   a. demonstrating the unimpaired physical capacities of the handicapped.
   *b. attitudinal change among camp staff toward the handicapped.
   c. reducing the degree of mental retardation of the campers.
   d. increasing the degree of dependence of the campers.

2. During debriefing in the camping program described in "Learning Through Outdoor Adventure Education," all of the following were accomplished *except*:
   a. asking each individual whether they enjoyed the activity.
   b. asking the group to identify what they had just done.
   c. asking whose ideas helped solve the problem.
   *d. asking who contributed most to solving the problem.

3. The major focus of Camp Riverwood described in "Learning Through Outdoor Adventure Education" is:
   *a. group participation in sports, movement and outdoor exploration.
   b. individual event competition.
   c. to train handicapped persons for the Special Olympics.
   d. leadership training for teachers of mentally retarded children.

True/False Questions

4. The campers who attended Camp Riverwood, described in "Learning Through Outdoor Adventure Education," were all from group homes or state residential institutions. (F)

5. According to "Learning Through Outdoor Adventure Education," recreational sports and movement activities are inherently reinforcing and promote learning, social interaction and greater self-reliance. (T)

GENERAL QUESTIONS

6. Discuss the goals of the program for the mentally retarded at Camp Riverwood described in "Learning Through Outdoor Adventure Education." Would the same goals be appropriate for other handicapped groups?
(greater physical, mental, emotional, and social awareness and growth; development of self-confidence and trust; improvement in socialization skills, interpersonal relationship skills, and level of independence; enhancement of verbal and nonverbal communication, physical mobility and coordination, and individual and group initiative)

7. The authors of "Learning Through Outdoor Adventure Education" describe self-reliance and group membership as two key constructs of the philosophy of Camp Riverwood. How do the activities of the camp try to combine these seemingly polar facets?
(group activities which require individual initiative; individual activities which require group support; comment within groups on individual contributions; comments within groups on examples of cooperation and mutual aid)

8. Discuss how the programs described in "Learning Through Outdoor Adventure Education" could be adapted for retarded children in a regular school environment.
(could be used in physical education classes, recess, morning opening exercises, or class breaks; could use material already available in schools; could use inside or outside spaces; new games, initiatives, and debriefing procedures easily adapted; rope course requires special equipment and training)

22. SPEAKING FOR THEMSELVES: A BIBLIOGRAPHY OF WRITINGS BY MENTALLY HANDICAPPED INDIVIDUALS,
KEITH E. STANOVICH AND PAULA J. STANOVICH
AE p. 110

ARTICLE SUMMARY

This brief summation argues for the importance of letting handicapped people, including the mentally retarded, speak for themselves as a means of educating others about their needs and abilities and dispelling prejudices. Several books, either written by or based on interviews with mentally retarded persons are described.

KEY TERMS AND TOPICS

Bibliography a description of books and other manuscripts relating to a given subject with notices of editions, dates of printing, and author(s).

CRITICAL ANALYSIS

Multiple Choice Questions

1. "The World of Nigel Hunt" described in the article "Speaking for Themselves," is a book by a man with:
   a. autism.
   b. multiple sclerosis.
   *c. Down syndrome.
   d. epilepsy.
2. The article "The Right to Self-Determination" described in the article "Speaking for Themselves," gives all the following as examples of demands of a group of retarded persons who conferred in Sweden in 1970 *except:*
   *a. mandatory summer camps for retarded adults.
   b. the right to marry.
   c. freedom of choice in determining vocations.
   d. banishment of the practice of having groups of retarded persons walk together through town.
3. According to "The Cloak of Competence" described in the article "Speaking for Themselves," the label rejected by many of the individuals who were discharged from state institutions during deinstitutionalization was the label:
   a. imbecile.
   b. feeble-minded.
   *c. retarded.
   d. idiot.

True/False Questions

4. According to "Speaking for Themselves," today there is a large body of literature authored by mentally handicapped individuals which is available to teachers, students, advocates, parents, and retardation workers. (F)
5. The authors of "Speaking for Themselves" feel it would be an exercise in futility to compare what mentally retarded persons say about themselves, to what is said about them by parents, professionals and the general public. (F)

GENERAL QUESTIONS

6. According to the article, "Speaking for Themselves," there are several reasons why it is important to let retarded individuals speak for themselves. What are some of these?
   (dispel myth that retarded people cannot speak for themselves; let retarded people appear as less different and more similar to rest of society; lift retarded people out of subordinate position; encourage society to listen to them and accept them as equals; learn more about the abuses perpetrated against retarded people; use opinions of retarded persons to redesign programs for them)
7. According to "Speaking for Themselves," why do you think professionals have always taken on the responsibility of speaking for retarded persons in the past, and to some extent still do today?
   (fear of what retarded persons might say; enjoyment of power of being able to speak for others; negative attitude toward retarded persons; poor education for retarded persons allowed few to learn to write as a means of speaking for themselves)
8. As explained in "Speaking for Themselves," because retarded persons have not been given the opportunity to speak on their own behalf, society tends to hold restricted views of their potential. Is this true of other handicapped persons as well? What handicapped groups have not been able to speak on their own behalf? What groups have?
   *(***have not:*** emotionally disturbed, multihandicapped, learning disabled; ***have:*** visually handicapped, orthopedically handicapped, health impaired, speech impaired)*

23. OUR MOST NEGLECTED NATURAL RESOURCE,
HAROLD C. LYON, JR.　　　　　　　　　　AE p. 116

ARTICLE SUMMARY

The author, head of the Office for the Gifted and Talented, US Department of Education, argues the importance of gifted children for society, evaluates the lack of attention to their needs historically and the current increase in such interest. He defines different categories of gifted children and suggests educational programs for them.

KEY TERMS AND TOPICS

Mentorships pairing of students with individuals in the community who are willing to share their experience in a particular field.
SEAs state education agencies.
LEAs local education agencies.
OGT US Department of Education's Office for the Gifted and Talented.

CRITICAL ANALYSIS

Multiple Choice Questions

1. According to the author of "Our Most Neglected Natural Resource," many gifted persons, when interviewed, point to which of the following as the single most important factor in their success?
   a. early childhood exposure to their field.
   b. solid elementary school education.
   c. proper secondary and professional training.
   *d. a mentor.
2. Gifted students, who remain at grade level with their peers without any special education, may take all of the following pathways, according to the author of "Our Most Neglected Natural Resource," *except:*
   a. concealing their ability.
   *b. showing off to teachers and peers.
   c. becoming discipline problems.
   d. becoming lethargic and apathetic.
3. According to "Our Most Neglected Natural Resource," the US Government began a wavering degree of commitment to the education of gifted students after what historical event?
   *a. launching of the Russian space satellite, Sputnik, in 1957.
   b. John Glenn's orbiting of the earth in 1962.
   c. Martin Luther King's leading of the Selma freedom march in 1965.
   d. signing of the Viet Nam peace agreement in 1973.

True/False Questions

4. Gifted and talented students are most likely to be males who come from white, affluent, northern European background families, says "Our Most Neglected Natural Resource." (F)
5. "Our Most Neglected Natural Resource" states that the 1969 Marland Report, a study of gifted education in America, was responsible for the formation of the Office of the Gifted and Talented (OGT) in 1972. (T)

GENERAL QUESTIONS

6. Why does the author of "Our Most Neglected Natural Resource" advocate a 5% cutoff for defining the gifted school-age population? What possible problems can you see with such a definition?
   *(***reason given:*** need to define a population that is noticeably different to establish public acceptance of gifted education; ***problems:*** admittedly arbitrary; appears to define many as ungifted; does not create broad base of parental support)*

7. What traits are presented in "Our Most Neglected Natural Resource" as characteristic of successful teachers and what evidence is presented for that view?
   (genuineness, emphathic understanding, and prizing [the opposite of apathy]; significantly higher achievement scores for students with empathetic teachers; and much more smiling in class)
8. What reason is emphasized in "Our Most Neglected Natural Resource" for providing special education for talented and gifted students? Is this an appropriate educational criterion?
   (reason is need of society for their human potential; the question is, should social or individual need determine educational policy?)

24. MEETING THE NEEDS OF GIFTED PRESCHOOLERS,
ANN E. LUPKOWSKI AND ELIZABETH A. LUPKOWSKI   AE p. 120

ARTICLE SUMMARY

This article is a scholarly discussion of the identification of, and enrichment strategies for, gifted preschool children. The authors contend that parent reports and observations must supplement standardized tests to identify young gifted children. Once found, these children need to be encouraged to develop their own uniqueness.

KEY TERMS AND TOPICS

Standardized Intelligence Tests intelligence tests that have been developed using large numbers of subjects for comparative purposes to develop performance norms for age.
Giftedness above-average ability in general intellectual ability, specific academic aptitude, leadership ability, creative or productive thinking, visual and performing arts, or psychomotor ability.

CRITICAL ANALYSIS
Multiple Choice Questions
1. All of the following are listed as characteristic areas of giftedness by the authors of "Meeting the Needs of Gifted Preschoolers" *except:*
   a. leadership ability.
   b. creative or productive thinking.
   c. specific academic aptitude.
   *d. multi-linguistic proficiency.
2. The authors of "Meeting the Needs of Gifted Preschoolers" suggested that parents' reports on their children can be elicited using all of the following formats *except:*
   a. rating scales.
   b. questionnaires.
   c. interviews.
   *d. standardized IQ tests.
3. According to "Meeting the Needs of Gifted Preschoolers," the ideal teacher for young, gifted children should be:
   a. structured and authoritarian.
   b. trained in psychobiology and neurophysiology.
   *c. flexible and accepting of uniqueness.
   d. able to respond with appropriate reinforcers for each new achievement.

True/False Questions
4. According to "Meeting the Needs of Gifted Preschoolers," on standardized IQ tests, gifted young children may show peaks of extraordinary high performance in some areas, but not necessarily in all cognitive ability areas. (T)
5. "Meeting the Needs of Gifted Preschoolers" states that programs for gifted preschoolers should emphasize individualization and independence in learning. (T)

GENERAL QUESTIONS
6. The authors of "Meeting the Needs of Gifted Preschoolers" stated that standardized IQ tests may not reveal giftedness in preschoolers. What are some of the reasons they gave for this belief?
   (tests are only partially reliable before the age of 5 or 6; preschoolers have short attention spans; tested child may be uncomfortable in testing situation with strange surroundings and unfamiliar people; child may play games with test materials; young children have difficulty expressing themselves verbally)
7. According to "Meeting the Needs of Gifted Preschoolers," what are some of the characteristics which might differentiate intellectually gifted preschoolers from their less gifted peers?
   (longer attention span; creativity; advanced social skills for their age; advanced number concepts; advanced verbal skills; exceptional memories; in-depth interests; attention to detail; high energy level; advanced reasoning ability; exceptional insight)
8. Based on your reading of "Meeting the Needs of Gifted Preschoolers," what types of activities should a preschool enrichment program for gifted children include? What types of activities should be avoided?
   (**include:** informal lessons; discovery learning; open-endedness; group interaction; independent learning; self-directed learning; **avoid:** formal lessons; mastery of all areas of curriculum; repetition of each new task until it is mastered; punishment for failure to perform tasks)

25. GIFTED/LEARNING DISABLED STUDENTS: THEIR POTENTIAL MAY BE BURIED TREASURE,
MARCIA P. WEILL   AE p. 124

ARTICLE SUMMARY

This scholarly article describes gifted/learning disabled persons from a historical perspective and also in terms of current identification and remediation. The author contends that many G/LD students remain unrecognized due to their compensating skills. This may constitute an enormous loss to our society.

KEY TERMS AND TOPICS

Gifted/Learning Disabled students who have an outstanding gift or talent and are capable of high performance but who also have a learning disorder that makes this achievement difficult.
Compensating Skills skills in which one attempts to achieve or win respect or prestige as a substitute for inability to achieve in some other skill area.

CRITICAL ANALYSIS
Multiple Choice Questions
1. The author of "Gifted/Learning Disabled Students" suggested that G/LD students can be recognized by all of the following academic characteristics *except:*
   *a. score of over 130 points on standardized IQ test.
   b. a tendency to ponder and react slowly.
   c. difficulty adapting to new routine.
   d. lack of self-esteem.
2. The eminent gifted/learning disabled persons described in "Gifted/Learning Disabled Students," such as Edison, Einstein, Rodin, and Patton, all had a disability in which area?
   a. written expression.
   *b. reading.
   c. calculation.
   d. spelling.
3. Maker (1982), cited in Weill's article on "Gifted/Learning Disabled Students," sets forth several categories of gifted students with another concurrent handicap. Which is *not* one of these special categories?
   a. gifted/socially-emotionally disturbed.
   *b. gifted/mentally retarded.
   c. gifted/mobility impaired.
   d. gifted/sensorily handicapped.

True/False Questions

4. Gifted/learning disabled students achieving near grade level are not as apt to have their problems recognized and remediated as G/LD students who are low achievers, according to "Gifted/Learning Disabled Students." (T)
5. "Gifted/Learning Disabled Students" states that the Marland Report of 1972 broadened the concept of giftedness from only those students with superior intellect to also include those students with superior nonintellective abilities. (T)

GENERAL QUESTIONS

6. The author of "Gifted/Learning Disabled Students," gave several examples of ways in which G/LD students circumvent their learning disability by using compensating skills. What are some of these?
(may learn to spell "by ear"; memorize whole pages of a reader; use superior reasoning ability; develop a basic sight vocabulary; pick up cues from sentence structure, syllabication, or context to guess what is in text)
7. According to "Gifted/Learning Disabled Students," if gifted/learning disabled students learn enough productive coping mechanisms and compensatory skills to achieve near grade level, why should we bother to try to identify them?
(harder to use compensatory skills as student gets older; G/LD student still feels frustrated not being able to learn the same way as others; LD leads to poor self-esteem; when compensatory skills fail, student may become withdrawn or aggressive; loss to society of potential gifts of G/LD)
8. Many handicapping conditions such as gifted/learning disabled cannot be discovered with standardized IQ tests. What are other methods mentioned in "Gifted/Learning Disabled Students" which can be used to assess children with special talents and special needs?
(patterns of academic strengths and weaknesses; talent checklists; interviews; parent reports; performance observations)

26. THE TEACHER AS COUNSELOR FOR THE GIFTED, JOYCE VAN-TASSEL-BASKA   AE p. 127

ARTICLE SUMMARY

This is an article for teachers who have gifted students in their classes. It argues that gifted students have special affective development needs which are rarely met by school counselors but which teachers can help to meet through individual and group work with the students.

KEY TERMS AND TOPICS

Counseling for the Gifted the provision of guidance for the personal, social, and educational development of an individual.

CRITICAL ANALYSIS
Multiple Choice Questions

1. Which of the following is listed in "The Teacher as Counselor for the Gifted" as a factor making mentorship and internship difficult to provide?
   a. lack of school system support.
   b. lack of interest on part of students.
   *c. time constraints.
   d. few available mentors or internship opportunities.
2. All but which of the following are suggested in "The Teacher as Counselor for the Gifted" as test-taking strategies to develop with gifted children?
   a. break the test item into parts.
   b. try some hypothetical items.
   *c. state the unknown.
   d. make a list.
3. In addition to leading in-class activities with gifted students, the author of "The Teacher as Counselor for the Gifted" believes a teacher should also:
   a. spend weekends entertaining her gifted protégés.

*b. act as an advocate with parents and other educational personnel.
   c. keep them after school for sensitivity training sessions.
   d. supervise summer counseling workshops for them.

True/False Questions

4. The author of "The Teacher as Counselor for the Gifted" believes that special counseling for gifted students should be an essential part of their school program from the time they enter kindergarten until they leave as graduated seniors. (T)
5. According to "The Teacher as Counselor for the Gifted," gifted students never feel inadequate. (F)

GENERAL QUESTIONS

6. The author of "The Teacher as Counselor for the Gifted" argues that the gifted have special affective needs. What needs are identified?
(integration of self; understanding differentness yet recognizing similarities to others; accepting and giving criticism; toleration of self and others; understanding strengths and weaknesses; skills that nurture both cognitive and affective development)
7. After reading "The Teacher as Counselor for the Gifted," in what ways, if any, do you think the affective needs of gifted students are different from those of other students?
(getting attention by poor behavior; keeping a low profile to avoid appearing too different; social withdrawal from peers; need to deal with parents around preoccupations with reading, etc.)
8. The article "The Teacher as Counselor for the Gifted" recommends that the teacher of the gifted may have the skills and be in the best position to counsel gifted students. What basis is given for this argument and how do you evaluate it?
(the lack of other counseling available and lack of training for counselors to deal with gifted; teacher already knows students; teacher of gifted familiar with their needs; working with a group of gifted students often best counseling mode; guidance can be integrated into ongoing activities)

27. CURRICULUM-BASED PROGRAMS FOR THE GIFTED, BYRON L. BARRINGTON   AE p. 133

ARTICLE SUMMARY

This is a scholarly article delineating the major issues facing gifted and talented education and suggesting curriculum-based programs in schools to help alleviate the problems. The author gives steps needed to implement curriculum-based education and several advantages of so doing.

KEY TERMS AND TOPICS

Curriculum-Based Program special educational program which gives supplemental materials and differential assignments to special needs students within the curriculum being taught at that time to the regular class.
Gifted Underachiever a student with superior intellectual abilities in one or more subject areas or with superior nonintellectual talents in one or more areas who fails to perform in the area of giftedness and is unresponsive to education in general.

CRITICAL ANALYSIS
Multiple Choice Questions

1. According to the author of "Curriculum-Based Programs for the Gifted," when a gifted and talented program requires that G/T students work at tasks unrelated to the curriculum of the regular class, the result is typically:
   *a. teacher resentment.
   b. G/T student resentment.
   c. relief on the part of the regular class.
   d. relief on the part of the teacher.

2. The author of "Curriculum-Based Programs for the Gifted" feels that gifted and talented students for curriculum-based programs are best identified through:
   a. IQ tests.
   b. judgment of the G/T student's parents.
   c. peer nominations.
   *d. achievement in each curriculum area.
3. According to "Curriculum-Based Programs for the Gifted," a curriculum-based program for gifted and talented students will have most difficulty implementing a curriculum to teach ___ to G/T children.
   a. science
   *b. creativity
   c. art
   d. social studies

True/False Questions

4. According to the author of "Curriculum-Based Programs for the Gifted," lack of challenge is seldom a deficiency in the primary grades for gifted students. (F)
5. According to "Curriculum-Based Programs for the Gifted," gifted students excel in all subject areas and seldom fall below grade level in any of them. (F)

GENERAL QUESTIONS

6. The author of "Curriculum-Based Programs for the Gifted" addresses four issues facing gifted and talented education today. What are these major concerns?
   (inadequate challenge; insufficient opportunity for G/T students to interact with real peers; lack of continuity in G/T programming from K-12; inadequate recognition of the accomplishments of G/T students)
7. What are some of the advantages of the curriculum-based program for G/T education described in "Curriculum-Based Programs for the Gifted"? What are two disadvantages?
   (**advantages:** *keep G/T students interested in learning by matching pace and content to their abilities; provide extra stimulation only in those curricula areas in which their abilities are superior; easier for teachers; easier to identify G/T by curriculum area; more interaction with real peers; more continuity of education from K-12;* **disadvantages:** *no emphasis on stimulation of creativity or leadership; does not identify the gifted underachiever)*
8. According to "Curriculum-Based Programs for the Gifted," must the school be responsible for developing all the special skills of gifted and talented students? What community resources can assist in G/T education? How can family help?
   (**community resources:** *theater groups, music lessons, art classes, boy or girl scouts, religious groups, nature clubs or camps, sports teams, AFS program, hobby clubs, Big Brothers/Big Sisters, volunteer jobs;* **family:** *take children to zoos, museums, concerts, plays, sporting events, help children get involved in community activities)*

28. A "SOCIAL" SOCIAL STUDIES MODEL FOR GIFTED STUDENTS,
DIANE E. WILLARD   AE p. 136

ARTICLE SUMMARY

This article by a teacher of gifted elementary school students applies the ideas of John Dewey to the development of programs for gifted children and describes in detail the development of one class in social studies for gifted elementary school children.

KEY TERMS AND TOPICS

Social shared activity.
Web a relationship diagram showing the relation of various topics to a question under consideration.

CRITICAL ANALYSIS
Multiple Choice Questions

1. In the social studies class described in "A 'Social' Social Studies Model for Gifted Students," all but which of the following were described as factors that students discovered were necessary for successful community service projects?
   a. careful attention to detail.
   b. delegation of responsibility.
   c. group cooperation.
   *d. strong adult guidance.
2. "Renzulli's Triad" as described in "A 'Social' Social Studies Model for Gifted Students" involves all but which of the following?
   a. exploratory activities.
   b. specific skills activities.
   c. problem-solving activities.
   *d. evaluation of own work.
3. The enrichment social studies class described in "A 'Social' Social Studies Model for Gifted Students" studied all of the following *except:*
   a. economics and urbanization.
   b. the nature of culture.
   *c. democracy in education.
   d. social organization and adaptation.

True/False Questions

4. The social studies program for the gifted described in "A 'Social' Social Studies Model for Gifted Students" took place over two years for 7th and 8th graders. (F)
5. According to "A 'Social' Social Studies Model for Gifted Students," John Dewey believed that shared activity is the greatest of human goods. (T)

GENERAL QUESTIONS

6. The author of "A 'Social' Social Studies Model for Gifted Students" draws on the ideas of John Dewey, a once-revered but more recently disparaged philosopher and educational theorist. What ideas does she take from Dewey and how would you evaluate their use?
   (concept of "social" as shared activity; valuing of shared activity; belief in freedom of intelligence; concept of experience as key to education; concept of problem solving; education as a social process; classroom as a microcosm of the broader process of social learning)
7. The program described in "A 'Social' Social Studies Model for Gifted Students" describes a class in which the direction is given primarily by students' interests and active explorations, in which the content and outcome of classes could not have been known in advance by the teacher. What do you consider the pros and cons of such an approach?
   (**pro:** *more exciting for students and teacher; students motivated by their interests; draws on and stimulates creativity; skills and self-discipline develop out of students' own needs and drives;* **con:** *does not guarantee completion of standard curriculum; lack of good organization and focus of learning; may not teach skills students need but aren't interested in acquiring; requires high level of flexibility and involvement from teacher)*
8. Do you think the approach described in "A 'Social' Social Studies Model for Gifted Students" is applicable only to gifted and talented students? Why?
   (**yes:** *need of most students for more direction; lack of intense motivation from strong interests; greater need for skills development;* **no:** *stimulating effect on students' interests; positive effect on self-image; ability to draw out and develop otherwise unrecognized talents)*

29. EDUCATOR PERCEPTIONS OF BEHAVIOR PROBLEMS OF MAINSTREAMED STUDENTS,
N. JO CAMPBELL, JUDITH E. DOBSON, AND JANE M. BOST   **AE p. 142**

ARTICLE SUMMARY

This article reports on a study of teachers' and other educators' attitudes toward various types of students. It finds different interpretations of the severity of behavioral problems and different kinds of teacher reponse recommended for mentally handicapped, physically handicapped, and nonhandicapped students.

KEY TERMS AND TOPICS

Behavior Problem a pattern of behavior which deviates from the norm of social interaction for the given situation.

CRITICAL ANALYSIS

Multiple Choice Questions

1. In "Educator Perceptions of Behavior Problems of Mainstreamed Students," the educators surveyed regarded the same behavioral problem as less serious when it was presented by:
   a. a male.
   b. a physically handicapped student.
   *c. a mentally handicapped student.
   d. a nonhandicapped student.
2. In "Educator Perceptions of Behavior Problems of Mainstreamed Students," the educators surveyed were likely to recommend more authoritarian treatments for behavior problems of:
   a. females.
   *b. nonhandicapped students.
   c. physically handicapped students.
   d. mentally handicapped students.
3. All of the following were offered as explanations of why teachers perceive the behaviors of different classifications of students as more serious or less serious in "Educator Perceptions of Behavior Problems of Mainstreamed Students," *except:*
   *a. whether different sex hormones make the behavior inevitable.
   b. whether the student has the capacity to "know better."
   c. teachers expect different behaviors from children in different classifications.
   d. teacher expectations of behaviors help determine actual behaviors.

True/False Questions

4. As mentioned in "Educator Perceptions of Behavior Problems of Mainstreamed Students," according to several recent Gallup polls, the number one concern regarding education in the United States is discipline in the schools. (T)
5. According to "Educator Perceptions of Behavior Problems of Mainstreamed Students," special education teachers are now required to teach students with severe behavior problems who, ten years ago, would have been taught by teachers in the regular classroom. (F)

GENERAL QUESTIONS

6. What do you think are the strengths and weaknesses of the research presented in "Educator Perceptions of Behavior Problems of Mainstreamed Students"?
   (**strengths:** *attempt to look at a question hardly ever studied; came up with statistically significant results;* **weaknesses:** *representativeness of sample unclear; measures paper response rather than actual behavioral response of teachers)*
7. "Educator Perceptions of Behavior Problems of Mainstreamed Students" advances the hypothesis that "inappropriate behaviors of mentally handicapped students in the mainstreamed environment is perpetuated by educators who have not internalized information for working with handicapped

children." On what do they base this and how do you evaluate their argument?
   (based on less severity attributed to teachers in study to behavior problems of handicapped, and the tendency to respond to them in less authoritarian fashion; this is interpreted as lower expectation for their behavior, which may in turn lower student's expectation for his own behavior)
8. The authors of "Educator Perceptions of Behavior Problems of Mainstreamed Students" cite research findings that punishment is generally ineffective and may even lead to further behavioral problems. If this research were confirmed, what implications would it have for schools?
   (research on developing alternatives to punishment; retraining of teachers; reorientation of public)

30. THE NORTH CAROLINA EXPERIENCE,
LENORE BEHAR   **AE p. 147**

ARTICLE SUMMARY

This descriptive article details the solution that North Carolina found for providing services to seriously disturbed, assaultive children after a successful class action lawsuit against the state provided the problem: routine institutionalization of disturbed children fails to meet the mandates of PL 94-142.

KEY TERMS AND TOPICS

Class Action Lawsuit legal decision that provides that action taken on behalf of complainant applies not only to the individual but also to all members of the class to which that individual belongs.
Willie M. Population all seriously disturbed children, similarly situated to the four minors who won the Willie M. class action lawsuit against North Carolina, who have been denied appropriate treatment and education.
Individualized Service Plan a program for rehabilitation written for every unique individual belonging to the Willie M. population in North Carolina that describes his/her goals, services needed, and suggested methods for obtaining them.
Respite Services a temporary suspension of the planned program with someone else providing emergency care until the regular services can be resumed.

CRITICAL ANALYSIS

Multiple Choice Questions

1. The model for child mental health services described in the article "The North Carolina Experience" was developed primarily for children who are:
   *a. violent.
   b. neglected or abused.
   c. alcohol and other substance abusers.
   d. suicidal.
2. Five years after "The North Carolina Experience" was implemented, the adjudication of the majority of cases of juveniles found guilty of criminal behaviors was to:
   *a. community habilitation programs.
   b. training schools.
   c. psychiatric hospitals.
   d. minimum security prisons.
3. The persons given most credit in the description of "The North Carolina Experience" for making the system work were the:
   a. children involved in the program.
   b. parents of the children involved in the program.
   c. staff of the residential institutions.
   *d. case managers of the child clients.

True/False Questions

4. The population served by the program described in "The North Carolina Experience," was comprised predominantly of young black males from detention facilities, training schools or child care institutions. (F)
5. In "The North Carolina Experience," the North Carolina project's philosophy was that children are best served close to

their own communities to maximize the possibility of family involvement. (T)

GENERAL QUESTIONS

6. The "Willie M" class action lawsuit against the State of North Carolina came about because of the State's failure to provide appropriate treatment and education for Willie. What are some of the reasons given in "The North Carolina Experience" for the failure to provide such services?
(absence of treatment programs; absence of individualized educational programs; lack of linkages between various service agencies; attitude on the part of North Carolina professionals that such students were untreatable)

7. The author of "The North Carolina Experience" states that juvenile justice training schools are not appropriate settings for the provision of needed treatment services for juvenile offenders. Why? Give several pros and cons of training schools.
*(**pro**: protect the community from the risk of having such a juvenile living among them; training school can provide very highly specialized services not available in most communities; **con**: removal of child to training school also removes child from family and community and vice versa and creates new problems of reintegration when child leaves training school; training school is highly restrictive and does not approach life as it is lived outside; no individualized service plan for each child in a training school)*

8. According to "The North Carolina Experience," what are some advantages of community-based individualized service plans?
(statement of needs is based on real needs, not on what is available in training school; services may be obtained from several community resources; each child can be rehabilitated in creative manner; family and community members involved in habilitation; less costly; case management is more personal and responsive; program can be modified as needed without red tape; child becomes more employable)

31. CHILD ABUSE AND NEGLECT,
JEROME E. LEAVITT   AE p. 153

ARTICLE SUMMARY

This article is a summary of an interview with Jolly K., co-founder of Parents Anonymous. It discusses the prevalence of child abuse and neglect, the various types, how teachers can identify abused and neglected children, and what they should do if they suspect abuse or neglect.

KEY TERMS AND TOPICS

Physical Abuse includes beating, shaking, and burning.
Sexual Abuse includes harassment, fondling, sodomy or intercourse.
Physical Neglect includes abandonment, leaving children unsupervised, failing to house, feed, clothe, or provide medical assistance.
Emotional Abuse verbal harassment, refusing to speak to children, shifting between massive affection and mistreatment, unrealistic pressure.

CRITICAL ANALYSIS
Multiple Choice Questions

1. The author of "Child Abuse and Neglect" gives all of the following as reasons for the increase of child abuse *except:*
   a. more reporting of incidents.
   b. abusive persons more frequently in home due to unemployment.
   c. parents more often take out frustrations on vulnerable, convenient children.
   *d. more societal approval for violence against children.

2. The author of "Child Abuse and Neglect" reported that ___ accounts for the largest number of cases.
   a. physical abuse
   b. sexual abuse

   *c. physical neglect
   d. emotional abuse

3. According to "Child Abuse and Neglect," persons making reports of child abuse:
   *a. are protected from civil liability.
   b. are subject to being sued.
   c. should first receive approval from their principal or other administrator.
   d. are usually troublemakers trying to get revenge on persons in their family or neighborhood.

True/False Questions

4. According to "Child Abuse and Neglect," unlike Alcoholics Anonymous which has had a high success rate, Parents Anonymous had had a low rate of success in preventing future incidents of child abuse and neglect. (F)

5. "Child Abuse and Neglect" states that school systems should not get involved in the reporting of suspected child abuse and neglect. (F)

GENERAL QUESTIONS

6. What is the impact in the article "Child Abuse and Neglect" of having a member of Parents Anonymous as a spokesperson on abuse and neglect?
(provides an alternative to a professional's perspective; implies inside understanding of abusive parents' condition and situation; assures personal concern; may ignore professional perspectives that would be relevant)

7. According to "Child Abuse and Neglect," what can teachers contribute to dealing with abuse and neglect? Do you agree?
(help identify abused and neglected children; file reports where appropriate; refer parents for help; help children find ways to deal with problems without violence and become familiar with young children so they will be better parents themselves)

8. According to "Child Abuse and Neglect," what are some of the reasons that child abuse and neglect are increasing?
(increase in reporting; unemployment and resulting elevated stress; presence of parent(s) in home; loss of outside role and support network)

32. HOW TO REACH THE UNDERACHIEVER,
SYLVIA B. RIMM   AE p. 155

ARTICLE SUMMARY

This article is of special interest to teachers faced with the problem of helping children who began school with high achievement and IQ test scores but then began underachieving, to regain the motivation needed to succeed. The author classifies underachievers as either dependent or dominant and suggests different ways to help each type.

KEY TERMS AND TOPICS

Dependent Underachiever an academically capable student who performs poorly in school because of a failure to take responsibility or organize tasks efficiently.
Dominant Underachiever an academically capable student who performs poorly in school because of a need to feel in control and an inability to cope with defeat.

CRITICAL ANALYSIS
Multiple Choice Questions

1. According to "How to Reach the Underachiever," all of the following behaviors are characteristic of academic underachievers *except:*
   a. poor self-concepts.
   *b. consistently poor school work.
   c. disorganization.
   d. daydreaming during school.

2. According to the article "How to Reach the Underachiever," academic underachievement may be learned as a result of

several difficult family interactions. These patterns include all of the following *except:*

  *a. being an only child.

  b. early illness of child.

  c. parents' marital problems.

  d. one parent being away from home for an extended time.

3. According to the author of "How to Reach the Underachiever," the "attention addiction" of a dependent underachiever should be met with:

  a. sympathy.

  b. one-to-one instruction.

  c. cold turkey withdrawal of all attention.

  *d. standing back and permitting the child to struggle through the task.

True/False Questions

4. According to "How to Reach the Underachiever," most underachievers begin school with high achievement and IQ test scores. (T)

5. According to the author of "How to Reach the Underachiever," an underachiever often spends time manipulating others in order to hide a poor self-concept. (T)

GENERAL QUESTIONS

6. The author of "How to Reach the Underachiever" wrote that the main characteristic that distinguishes achievers from underachievers is the way in which they cope with competition. Explain how each group, dependent underachievers and dominant underachievers, cope with competition in faulty ways. *(dependent underachiever: fails to organize self to accomplish task; daydreams; waits for help; cries; dominant underachiever: manipulates others to do work; gets angry and/or pouts rather than attacking task; talks during class; fools around rather than working)*

7. According to "How to Reach the Underachiever," what could be some of the factors in early childhood and primary school years that contribute to a child's becoming a dominant underachiever? *(every task completed successfully with no early experiences of failure; parents model perfectionism; child reinforced for seeking attention continually; child reinforced for wielding power and dominance; child rewarded for independent behaviors; child seldom told no; child seldom disciplined)*

8. According to "How to Reach the Underachiever," how can teachers differentiate an underachiever from a child with a learning disability? Do you think that some LD children are incorrectly classified as underachievers? Could some underachievers be misclassified as learning disabled? *(differentiation is accomplished most accurately by using several measures such as standardized tests, observations, parent interviews, school records, projective tests, teacher reports, interview with student; misclassifications occur both ways; many students are both LD and underachievers)*

33. REDUCING STRESS OF STUDENTS IN CONFLICT, ELIZABETH DUFFNER, NICHOLAS J. LONG, AND STANLEY A. FAGAN   **AE p. 158**

ARTICLE SUMMARY

This article argues that there is a considerable amount that teachers can do to help troubled children under stress, even if that stress originates outside the school situation. It describes eight teacher strategies to provide such help.

KEY TERMS AND TOPICS

Stress strain, pressure, or any tension exerted upon a person that tends to alter normal behavior patterns and physiological functioning.

CRITICAL ANALYSIS

Multiple Choice Questions

1. All but which of the following are benefits which "Reducing Stress of Students in Conflict" claims result when students are able to express their emotions and have them accepted by an adult:

  a. physical and psychological relief.

  b. a sense of normalcy.

  c. a relationship of trust.

  *d. an alternative to familial support.

2. Which of the following is suggested in "Reducing Stress of Students in Conflict" as a way teachers can lower pressure for children under stress?

  a. allowing them to go home early.

  b. allowing them to stay after school to provide a break from a disrupted home.

  *c. temporarily lowering academic requirements.

  d. providing assignments at which they know the students can do well.

3. "Reducing Stress of Students in Conflict" states that having students in conflict help other less fortunate students is beneficial for all of the following reasons *except:*

  *a. giving them someone to commiserate with about how cruel life is.

  b. helping them observe coping skills of others.

  c. enhancing the helping student's sense of self-worth.

  d. the helping process focuses on the present and future, not the past.

True/False Questions

4. According to "Reducing Stress of Students in Conflict," psychological conditions which children face tend to remain static or fixed over time. (F)

5. "Reducing Stress of Students in Conflict" explains that all children experience stress in school at various times. (T)

GENERAL QUESTIONS

6. What answers do the authors of "Reducing Stress of Students in Conflict" give to the belief that teachers can give little help to students whose emotional problems are rooted outside the school context? *(teachers can adjust level of classroom stress; promote skills for coping with stress; provide some personal acceptance for student; provide a successful experience which creates a basis for trust in adults; can help keep the student's outside problems from being transformed into school problems long enough for the external problems to improve)*

7. How do the authors of "Reducing Stress of Students in Conflict" suggest that teachers orient students regarding disappointment and failure? *(emphasize that they are not due to student's "badness" or wrongdoing; make clear that a certain amount of hostility from others is normal; helping student accept defeat by acknowledging its pain for the student; trying to find some value or benefit even in a disappointing experience; communicating faith in the student's ability to endure the frustration)*

8. What advantages do the authors of "Reducing Stress of Students in Conflict" present as resulting from encouraging students to help others who are even less fortunate than themselves? *(realization that there are others whose problems are even worse; awareness of their coping skills; enhanced feelings of self-worth; lowered need for self-deprecation; increases focus on present and future rather than past)*

34. EFFECT OF TEACHER TRAINING SESSIONS ON LISTENER PERCEPTION OF VOICE DISORDERS,
NICHOLAS J. DEGREGORIO AND NANCY G. POLOW
AE p. 164

ARTICLE SUMMARY

The authors of this article contend that many students with voice disorders are neither assessed nor offered remedial services due to a lack of information about them. An in-service program is described which can be used to train teachers to recognize students with voice disorders.

KEY TERMS AND TOPICS

Voice Disorder a communication disorder which involves the pitch, the loudness, or the quality (e.g., nasality) of speech.
Voice Intensity amount of strength used to produce sounds.
Vocal Nasality degree to which sounds are emitted through the nasal cavity.
Vocal Resonation degree to which sounds emitted vibrate.
Pitch the frequency of vibrations which determine sounds from low to high.
Vocal Range limits of sounds which can be produced from lowest pitch to highest pitch.

CRITICAL ANALYSIS
Multiple Choice Questions

1. According to the authors of "Effect of Teacher Training Sessions on Listener Perception of Voice Disorders," one of the more common and unrecognized voice disorders in primary school children is:
   *a. hoarseness.
   b. stuttering.
   c. lisping.
   d. delayed speech.
2. The voice profile rating sheets described in "Effect of Teacher Training Sessions on Listener Perception of Voice Disorders" rated voice parameters of:
   a. omissions and additions.
   b. distortions and stammering.
   *c. intensity and resonance.
   d. spasticity and aphonia.
3. Compared to the control group, the experimental group of teachers who had had the training described in the article "Effect of Teacher Training Sessions on Listener Perception of Voice Disorders," made significantly fewer errors in judging:
   a. vocal range.
   b. severity of problem.
   c. cluttering.
   *d. nasality.

True/False Questions

4. Even after the training sessions described in "Effect of Teacher Training Sessions on Listener Perception of Voice Disorders," teachers found it very difficult to determine if a child's voice was resonating or not. (F)
5. According to "Effect of Teacher Training Sessions on Listener Perception of Voice Disorders," elementary school teachers hold the major responsibility for the rehabilitation of a child's voice disorder. (F)

GENERAL QUESTIONS

6. The article on the "Effect of Teacher Training Sessions on Listener Perception of Voice Disorders" told how the researchers increased teachers' awareness of voice problems. Describe the content of the training sessions.
   (general background information; definitions of voice disorders; explanations of vocal rating sheets; samples of voice disorders presented along with information on how to rate on rating sheet; vocal abuse explained; practice given rating taped samples of voice disorders)
7. According to the authors of "Effect of Teacher Training Sessions on Listener Perception of Voice Disorders," why is it

important for teachers to do preliminary diagnosis of voice disorders or other communication disorders of their students and refer them for further diagnostic measures?
   (speech-language clinician does not hear all children in class speak on regular basis; parents are so habituated to way their child speaks, they may not recognize any problem; physician may not hear child speak enough to make referral; unless referrals are made to speech-language clinicians, the problem may continue unabated or get worse)
8. Voice disorders are one of four general areas in which communication can be impaired; the other three are articulation, fluency, and language. Why did the authors of "Effect of Teacher Training Sessions on Listener Perception of Voice Disorders" concentrate on training teachers to recognize voice disorders?
   (parents, neighbors, health professionals or others are more apt to notice poor articulation, stuttering, or delayed speech or muteness; other problems get more referrals and treatment prior to elementary school; voice disorders are very common as well as unrecognized in the primary grades; teachers generally do not know very much about voice disorders)

35. ATTITUDES OF INTERDISCIPLINARY TEAM MEMBERS TOWARD SPEECH-LANGUAGE SERVICES IN PUBLIC SCHOOLS,
LOU TOMES AND DIXIE D. SANGER
AE p. 166

ARTICLE SUMMARY

The authors contend that many educators do not know how they can work together with speech-language clinicians to improve the communication skills of communication disordered children. The speech-language clinician and teachers should interact more, each providing input for the other's program.

KEY TERMS AND TOPICS

Speech-Language Clinician professional person educated to diagnose and remediate impairments of articulation, voice fluency, and language.

CRITICAL ANALYSIS
Multiple Choice Questions

1. The research reported in "Attitudes of Interdisciplinary Team Members Toward Speech-Language Services" surveyed the attitudes of all of the following interdisciplinary team members *except:*
   a. psychologists.
   b. principals.
   c. learning-disabilities teachers.
   *d. speech-language pathologists.
2. In the research reported in "Attitudes of Interdisciplinary Team Members Toward Speech-Language Services," the strongest disagreement came to which statement?
   a. The speech-language clinician offers appropriate suggestions for managing communication problems in classrooms.
   *b. The size of the speech-language clinician's caseload is too small to justify the professional position.
   c. As a team member, I provide sufficient input into the development of treatment programs for speech and language impaired students.
   d. The speech-language clinician provides in-services which help other staff personnel actively relate to speech-language impaired children.
3. A major recommendation of the authors of "Attitudes of Interdisciplinary Team Members Toward Speech-Language Services" was for more:
   a. special classes for speech-language impaired students.
   b. parental involvement in a child's speech-language therapy.
   c. students to be added to the caseload of each speech-language clinician.
   *d. in-service training sessions which address speech-language therapy.

True/False Questions

4. According to "Attitudes of Interdisciplinary Team Members Toward Speech-Language Services," for the most part, educators view speech-language clinicians and their programs positively. (T)
5. The authors of "Attitudes of Interdisciplinary Team Members Toward Speech-Language Services" feel that speech-language remediation helps children develop an improved self-concept and perform better in academics. (T)

GENERAL QUESTIONS

6. The authors of "Attitudes of Interdisciplinary Team Members Toward Speech-Language Services" recommended that speech-language clinicians have more interaction with teachers. What purposes did they say increased interaction would serve?
   (provide clinician with more information on how to manage children with communication disorders in their classrooms; improve teachers' attitude toward speech-language therapy; allow teachers to do preliminary screening for communication disorders; improve scheduling/time in therapy problems; keep teachers better informed about child's progress)
7. Language disability is one form of a developmental learning disability. According to "Attitudes of Interdisciplinary Team Members Toward Speech-Language Services," should a child with a language disability be given special remedial services by a learning-disability teacher or by a speech-language clinician? What are the advantages of therapy by each person? Should both professionals provide therapy?
   (L-D teacher: can keep child in class while providing services; can recognize and concurrently work with any other developmental learning disabilities; S-L clinician: can provide itinerant one-to-one special therapy; has more specialized knowledge of therapy for language disabilities; both: child gets more special attention; may confuse child if two professionals do not work closely together, or if they have conflicts about therapy)
8. What are the pros and cons of having one permanent speech-language clinician on the staff of every elementary school?
   (pro: number of communication disordered children is large and increasing; more interdisciplinary interaction and understanding; con: expensive; caseload may not be large enough; caseload may be too large for just one S-L clinician)

36. SOME WAYS TO HELP THE LANGUAGE-DEFICIENT CHILD IN THE CLASSROOM, THELMA ZIRKELBACH AND KATHRYN BLAKESLEY AE p. 171

ARTICLE SUMMARY

The authors contend that teachers frequently fail to recognize that academic failure may be primarily due to some language deficiency.

KEY TERMS AND TOPICS

Oral-Language Deficiency a lack of vocabulary and oral language skills relative to age mates: may be related to deficit auditory processing.

CRITICAL ANALYSIS
Multiple Choice Questions

1. According to the authors of "Some Ways to Help the Language-Deficient Child in the Classroom," which is the best way to help a child learn a new vocabulary word?
   *a. find a real-life example of the word.
   b. make child look word up in dictionary.
   c. make child write word and its definition repeatedly.
   d. find a picture which relates to the world.
2. A language-deficient child trying to retrieve a word from memory may appear to have which other communication disorder, according to "Some Ways to Help the Language-Deficient Child in the Classroom"?
   a. hoarseness.
   *b. stuttering.
   c. articulation disorder.
   d. hyponasality.
3. According to "Some Ways to Help the Language-Deficient Child in the Classroom," all of the following are problems associated with language-deficiency *except:*
   a. frequent grammatical errors.
   b. difficulty making inferences.
   *c. reading disabilities.
   d. social communication disorders.

True/False Questions

4. According to "Some Ways to Help the Language-Deficient Child in the Classroom," using synonyms will enhance the language-deficient child's understanding of a new vocabulary word. (T)
5. The authors of "Some Ways to Help the Language-Deficient Child in the Classroom" feel that brainstorming sessions are very detrimental to the self-concepts of language-deficient children. (F)

GENERAL QUESTIONS

6. The authors of "Some Ways to Help the Language-Deficient Child in the Classroom" gave several behavioral characteristics of these children. What are some of them?
   (difficulty learning new vocabulary; confused by multiple meanings of words; poor understanding of similarities and differences; can't retrieve words; poor verbal expression; do not make inferences from verbal information; make many grammatic errors; poor interpretation and response to social situations)
7. The authors of "Some Ways to Help the Language-Deficient Child in the Classroom" suggested several games which will help language-deficient children. Should these games be used with non-language-deficient children at the same time? What are the pros and cons of integrating these games into a mainstream classroom program?
   (pro: improves all children's vocabularies; deficient child's memory may be stimulated by hearing classmates produce words; language games provide children with idea that language is fun; non-language-deficient classmates are language role models for disabled child; con: language-deficient child may feel frustrated by inability to succeed at these games as quickly as classmates; classmates may ridicule deficient child for failure to participate or for mistaken participation)
8. Extensive drill is often necessary to help a language-deficient child. According to "Some Ways to Help the Language-Deficient Child in the Classroom," should this be accomplished in a mainstream class or in a more restrictive setting? Why?
   (mainstream: feel more normal; interact with normal children; special class: more individual attention; less chance of being ridiculed)

37. A MODEL FOR TRAINING AND USING COMMUNICATION ASSISTANTS, BEATRICE C. JIMENEZ AND DEE ANN ISEYAMA AE p. 173

ARTICLE SUMMARY

The article describes a model for training and using communication assistants to provide services to students with speech and language disorders. The steps include: orientation, demonstration, participation and implementation. These steps are explained and examples are provided.

KEY TERMS AND TOPICS

Communication Assistants parents, aids, and other personnel who have been trained to help provide remediation services to students with speech and language disorders.

CRITICAL ANALYSIS

Multiple Choice Questions

1. Which of the following is not one of the steps described in "A Model for Training and Using Communication Assistants"?
   a. implementation.
   b. participation.
   *c. identification.
   d. demonstration.

2. All of the following are responsibilities of the licensed speech-language pathologist, not the trained communication assistant, as described in "A Model for Training and Using Communication Assistants" *except:*
   *a. maintaining daily logs of therapy.
   b. report writing.
   c. making referrals to other professionals.
   d. determining when a student may end therapy.

3. The program described in "A Model for Training and Using Communication Assistants" was applied to which of the following populations?
   a. Head Start for Native American (Navajo) children.
   *b. Head Start for migrant workers' children.
   c. day care program for Vietnamese refugees' children.
   d. bilingual primary school program for Hispanic children.

True/False Questions

4. According to "A Model for Training and Using Communication Assistants," prior to receiving services for trained communication assistants, students should be screened and assessed for speech and language disorders by a licensed speech-language pathologist. (T)

5. "A Model for Training and Using Communication Assistants" asserts that each communication assistant is ready to begin participating in a child's speech-language therapy program after seven hours of training. (F)

GENERAL QUESTIONS

6. Describe the types of teaching that the speech-language pathologist provides during the demonstration phase of the model program described in "A Model for Training and Using Communication Assistants."
   (performs techniques with client that had been discussed with trainee during orientation; identifies clients' correct and incorrect responses; demonstrates all aspects of therapy; discusses therapy and answers trainees' questions after client has returned to regular classroom)

7. According to "A Model for Training and Using Communication Assistants," what are the pros and cons of training parents to help with their own child's therapy and with the therapy of their child's peers?
   (pro: *once techniques are learned parent can provide additional therapy outside of scheduled therapy sessions; parents become more aware of speech-language abilities and needs of their child and his/her friends; lightens SLP's case load and speeds remediation;* **con:** *child may not work as hard for parent as for SLP; parent may put undue pressure on child to remediate speech outside of therapy session; parent may gossip about speech-language problems of other children with whom they work)*

8. From your reading of "A Model for Training and Using Communication Assistants," for which other areas of exceptionality do you think day assistants can be trained to provide supplemental special services? For which areas do you think therapy should be left only to professionals?
   (trained assistants: *learning disabilites, mentally retarded, gifted, hearing impaired, visually impaired, orthopedically impaired, other health impaired, some behavior disorders;* **professionals:** *some types of emotional disorders)*

38. FUNCTIONAL APHONIA IN THE CHILD AND ADOLESCENT: THERAPEUTIC MANAGEMENT, SHARON L. MURRAY, MARY E. CARR, AND VIRGINIA JACOBS   AE p. 176

ARTICLE SUMMARY

This scholarly case study report presents five adolescents with functional aphonia. The authors trace the etiologies to psychological factors and describe treatments based on principles of psychotherapeutic management.

KEY TERMS AND TOPICS

Aphonia a loss of voice due to paralysis of the vocal cords.
Functional Aphonia loss of voice due to abduction of the vocal cords with no apparent physiological cause.

CRITICAL ANALYSIS

Multiple Choice Questions

1. The therapeutic management of the adolescents described in "Functional Aphonia in the Child and Adolescent" followed which approach most closely?
   a. implosive therapy approach.
   b. family therapy approach.
   c. systematic desensitization approach.
   *d. symptom-modification approach.

2. Throughout the therapies described in "Functional Aphonia in the Child and Adolescent," the speech-language pathologists did all of the following *except:*
   a. recognize how hard it is to regain voice.
   *b. ask the clients to recall the events immediately preceding the aphonia.
   c. remind the clients that normal voice is possible.
   d. support the clients' efforts to speak.

3. The four girls with functional aphonia described in "Functional Aphonia in the Child and Adolescent," had stresses related to all of the following *except:*
   a. family problems.
   b. academic achievement.
   *c. sexual inadequacy.
   d. peer interactions.

True/False Questions

4. According to "Functional Aphonia in the Child and Adolescent," functional aphonia is more common in middle-age women than it is in adolescent girls. (T)

5. The authors of "Functional Aphonia in the Child and Adolescent" state that functional aphonia is a form of malingering. (F)

GENERAL QUESTIONS

6. "Functional Aphonia in the Child and Adolescent" described a step-by-step process of therapy in initial contact with aphonic children. What were these steps?
   (achieve phonation through nonverbal sound as a cough; extend a vowel sound to the cough; chain vowels to the cough; add consonant sounds to vowels; add word sounds; repeat rote words such as counting or days of the week; imitate sentences of therapist; answer therapist's questions; make spontaneous conversation)

7. Functional aphonia may be an adaptive way for a person to respond to acute or chronic stress. What advantages can it confer? What are some disadvantages of being aphonic?
   (advantages: *gives a respite or "time out" from any form of communication; brings attention; provides an excuse for not fulfilling responsibilities;* **disadvantages:** *cannot express own wishes, likes, dislikes, etc.; often seen as a form of malingering or faking of illness)*

8. Aphonia is a communication disorder. According to "Functional Aphonia in the Child and Adolescent," it could also be classified as at least two other types of exceptionality. What are these?

Why do you think it is in the communication disorder classification?

(could be an emotional disorder or a health impairment; primary symptom is a communication disorder; therapy from speech-language pathologist can cure aphonia but other emotional disorder needs referral to psychotherapist; loss of voice can be due to laryngitis which can be cured with drugs but aphonia may continue for emotional reasons)

39. POOR LEARNING ABILITY...OR POOR HEARING?
LAWRENCE B. MOLLICK AND KENNETH S. ETRA
AE p. 182

ARTICLE SUMMARY

Hearing loss can be manifested in many types of classroom behavior, from intense attention to complete inattention. This article, addressed to classroom teachers, suggests ways of identifying children with hearing impairment, urges prompt examination of those with suspected loss, and indicates guidelines for teachers with hearing impaired students in their classrooms.

KEY TERMS AND TOPICS

Conductive Hearing Loss loss that comes from an impediment that interferes with transmission of sound inside the ear.
Allergic Salute a gesture of rubbing the palm of the hand upward over the mouth and nose which sometimes becomes habitual in children with allergies.

CRITICAL ANALYSIS
Multiple Choice Questions

1. According to "Poor Learning Ability...or Poor Hearing?" school children with impaired hearing may display all of the following classroom symptoms of this disorder *except:*
   *a. superior verbal skills.
   b. extreme attentiveness.
   c. profound inattentiveness.
   d. frequent colds.
2. According to "Poor Learning Ability...or Poor Hearing?" which of the following is *not* indicated as a common side effect of impaired hearing?
   a. delayed language development.
   b. poor reading ability.
   c. clumsiness.
   *d. reduced environmental exploration.
3. According to "Poor Learning Ability...or Poor Hearing?" what do teachers need to do to be heard more effectively by the hearing-impaired?
   a. emphasize vowels.
   *b. emphasize consonants.
   c. speak loudly.
   d. speak slowly.

True/False Questions

4. According to "Poor Learning Ability...or Poor Hearing?" hearing impaired children should be prevented from taking part in active sports if they wear hearing aids. (F)
5. "Poor Learning Ability...or Poor Hearing?" reveals that approximately one-half million American children between the ages of 6 and 12 suffer from hearing loss to some degree. (T)

GENERAL QUESTIONS

6. The authors of "Poor Learning Ability...or Poor Hearing?" counsel teachers that "if it is necessary to refer to the child's handicap, always do so in private, never in front of the class." Some other authorities urge that students' handicaps be dealt with openly and frankly in the classroom. What reasons could be given on each side and what is your opinion?
   (against discussion: avoid embarrassment; overcome self-consciousness; for discussion: define handicap as normal; educate other students for acceptance; encourage handicapped not to be embarrassed by condition)

7. Why, according to the article "Poor Learning Ability...or Poor Hearing?" are teachers likely to be the best people to recognize hearing problems?
   (spend many hours with children; work with children at a high level of awareness; in a position to notice subtle differences in response)
8. What signs might indicate a child with a hearing problem, according to "Poor Learning Ability...or Poor Hearing?"
   (abnormal attentiveness or inattentiveness; distorted speech; frequent colds and ear infections; allergies; a history of measles, mumps or rubella; reliance on gestures; signs of battering; requests for louder speech; inappropriate answers to questions)

40. TEACHERS' KNOWLEDGE OF, EXPOSURE TO, AND ATTITUDES TOWARD, HEARING AIDS AND HEARING AID WEARERS,
NORMAL J. LASS, JOHN E. TECCOC, AND CHARLES M. WOODFORD
AE p. 184

ARTICLE SUMMARY

This is a research-based report on teachers' knowledge about hearing aids. It lists areas where teachers should have more knowledge in order to assure that the aids worn by their mainstreamed students are functioning properly. It also suggests ways to improve teachers' attitudes toward hearing aid wearers.

KEY TERMS AND TOPICS

Hearing Impaired having a hearing disability making it difficult, but not impossible, to understand speech through the ears, with or without a hearing aid.
Hearing Aid a battery-powered device worn in or near the ear which amplifies the sounds and tones that are received through the auditory canal.

CRITICAL ANALYSIS
Multiple Choice Questions

1. The survey reported in "Teacher's Knowledge of, Exposure to, and Attitudes Toward, Hearing Aids and Hearing Aid Wearers" revealed that the majority of teachers do *not* know:
   a. that not everyone can benefit from a hearing aid.
   b. that a hearing aid does not cure a hearing impairment.
   c. that the size of a hearing aid is not related to how much amplification it provides.
   *d. where hearing aids can be purchased.
2. The statement about which teachers surveyed in "Teacher's Knowledge of, Exposure to, and Attitudes Toward, Hearing Aids and Hearing Aid Wearers" showed the most disagreement was:
   a. hearing aid wearers are as intelligent as non-hearing aid wearers.
   b. hearing aid wearers are socially more restricted.
   *c. people look older when they wear hearing aids.
   d. hearing aids are a worthwhile expense.
3. According to "Teacher's Knowledge of, Exposure to, and Attitudes Toward, Hearing Aids and Hearing Aid Wearers," the professional who assesses hearing and makes recommendations regarding the use of hearing aids is:
   *a. an audiologist.
   b. an acoustician.
   c. an otolaryngologist.
   d. an auricularist.

True/False Questions

4. "Teacher's Knowledge of, Exposure to, and Attitudes Toward, Hearing Aids and Hearing Aid Wearers" states that hearing aids should not be worn by children under five years of age. (F)
5. The overwhelming majority of the teachers who responded to the survey reported in "Teacher's Knowledge of, Exposure to, and Attitudes Toward, Hearing Aids and Hearing Aid Wearers"

had never had a course that included the topic of hearing aids. (T)

GENERAL QUESTIONS

6. The authors of "Teacher's Knowledge of, Exposure to, and Attitudes Toward, Hearing Aids and Hearing Aid Wearers" suggest that teachers of hearing impaired students should take continuing education courses on hearing aids and hearing aid wearers. What are some of the topics which should be included in these courses?
(structure and function of hearing aids; how to check the functioning of hearing aids; the role of the audiologist; facts versus myths about hearing aids and hearing aid wearers; principles of aural rehabilitation)

7. According to "Teacher's Knowledge of, Exposure to, and Attitudes Toward, Hearing Aids and Hearing Aid Wearers," what methods can be used to help teachers gain more information about hearing aids and hearing aid wearers if they cannot take a continuing education course on the subject?
(invite teachers to participate in sessions with child and audiologist; schedule conferences between teachers and audiologist; distribute hearing aid fact sheets or brochures to teachers; put posters on exhibits about hearing aids on display in schools; present slide show on hearing aids to teachers; give teachers a list of published resource materials on hearing aids)

8. As teachers have more and more handicapped students mainstreamed into regular classes, it becomes important that they know about many of the technological aids used by these students. What devices, as mentioned in "Teacher's Knowledge of, Exposure to, and Attitudes Toward, Hearing Aids and Hearing Aid Wearers," should teachers understand?
(FM systems for hearing-impaired; specialized canes for blind; braillewriters; Optacons; Kruzweil reading machines; microcomputers and various software for handicapped students; wheelchairs; braces; prosthetic devices, walkers)

41. SERVICE DELIVERY ALTERNATIVES FOR THE MAINSTREAMED HEARING-IMPAIRED CHILD,
DIANE BRACKETT AND ANTONIA BRANCIA MAXON
AE p. 187

ARTICLE SUMMARY

This report presents demographic and correlational data from a 6-year in-service training program to improve services to hearing impaired students in public schools. Three case histories are highlighted and suggestions are given for writing more appropriate IEPs.

KEY TERMS AND TOPICS

Self-Contained Classrooms full time special classes which serve the needs of one category of exceptionality (e.g., hearing impaired).
Mainstreamed Classrooms regular education classes which serve the needs of exceptional children alongside nonhandicapped students.
Sensorineural Hearing Loss a defect of the auditory nerve or the inner ear (semicircular canals, cochlea) which inhibits the transmission of auditory impulses to the brain.

CRITICAL ANALYSIS
Multiple Choice Questions

1. According to the authors of "Service Delivery Alternatives for the Mainstreamed Hearing-Impaired Child," annual assessments should be made on hearing impaired students in all of the following areas *except:*
   a. degree of hearing loss.
   *b. psychological status.
   c. academic achievement.
   d. communication skills.

2. The three students described in "Service Delivery Alternatives for the Mainstreamed Hearing-Impaired Child" had all of the following aids to education *except:*
   a. binaural hearing aids.
   *b. teletypewriters and printers.
   c. classroom FM systems.
   d. daily removal from mainstream classes for some special services.

3. According to "Service Delivery Alternatives for the Mainstreamed Hearing-Impaired Child," with which of the following school subjects would a hearing impaired child be most apt to have difficulties?
   a. math.
   b. spelling.
   *c. reading.
   d. art.

True/False Questions

4. As described in "Service Delivery Alternatives for the Mainstreamed Hearing-Impaired Child," a problem common to most hearing impaired students is decreased language proficiency. (T)

5. The 6-year demographic data described in "Service Delivery Alternatives for the Mainstreamed Hearing-Impaired Child" revealed that below grade 5, most hearing impaired children were in appropriate classes for their ages. (T)

GENERAL QUESTIONS

6. "Service Delivery Alternatives for the Mainstreamed Hearing-Impaired Child" recommended that the hearing impaired child's educational placement be reevaluated every year. They stated that a team decision should be made annually about future programming. What people should be part of this planning team?
(teachers, principal, audiologist, speech-language pathologist, school psychologist, members of any outside agencies that have evaluated or worked with student, parents, the student if he/she is old enough and wants to help plan program)

7. The authors of "Service Delivery Alternatives for the Mainstreamed Hearing-Impaired Child" suggested that a hearing impaired student's academic performance in a mainstreamed class depends on physical environment, classroom instruction, and communicative strategies. How can these three factors be modified to enhance the handicapped student's performance?
*(**physical environment:** FM system; preferential seating; check to be sure hearing aids are working; **classroom instruction:** writing key words on chalkboard; designating student speaking; restating student's comments; provision of a notetaker; **communicative strategies:** speech-language remediation; tutoring; resource room activities)*

8. According to "Service Delivery Alternatives for the Mainstreamed Hearing-Impaired Child," what are the advantages and disadvantages of having hearing impaired students in mainstream classes past grade 5?
*(**advantages:** interaction with hearing peers; self-concept as able and not disabled; **disadvantages:** may fall behind academically due to language disabilities; require more special services that teacher may not be providing)*

42. HEARING IMPAIRED STUDENTS IN REGULAR CLASSROOMS: A COGNITIVE MODEL FOR EDUCATIONAL SERVICES,
MANJULA B. WALDRON, THOMAS J. DIEBOLD, AND SUSAN ROSE
AE p. 192

ARTICLE SUMMARY

This is a scholarly article advancing the premise that visual and conceptual delivery of information presented in the classroom to hearing impaired students is more important than the verbal transliteration of the spoken material.

KEY TERMS AND TOPICS

Visual-Spatial Processing becoming aware of objects, qualities, or relations by means of input primarily from the senses of sight, touch, and movement.

Auditory Processing becoming aware of objects, qualities, or relations by means of input primarily from the sense of hearing.

CRITICAL ANALYSIS

Multiple Choice Questions

1. Three examples of visual delivery of information rather than auditory delivery were given in "Hearing Impaired Students in Regular Classrooms." They included all of the following *except:*
   *a. placing student front-row center during all oral presentations.
   b. showing science experiment with set of illustrations.
   c. pointing out math problem in book as teacher announces it.
   d. preparing each new vocabulary word on an index card with a picture, sign, and diacritical markings.
2. All of the following persons were asked to help adapt materials for visual delivery to hearing impaired students in the program described in "Hearing Impaired Students in Regular Classrooms" *except:*
   a. teacher of regular class.
   b. teacher of hearing impaired.
   *c. speech-language clinician.
   d. educational interpreter.
3. Visual presentations of materials helped the boy described in the case study in "Hearing Impaired Students in Regular Classrooms" improve his scores the most in which academic subject area?
   a. English.
   b. social studies.
   c. math.
   *d. science.

True/False Questions

4. According to "Hearing Impaired Students in Regular Classrooms," the best instructional format with deaf students is predominantly oral. (F)
5. As stated in "Hearing Impaired Students in Regular Classrooms," maximum gains are made by hearing impaired students when their interpreters stop transposing speech to sign and instead transpose speech to finger spelling. (F)

GENERAL QUESTIONS

6. The case study of the gifted/hearing impaired 13-year-old boy in "Hearing Impaired Students in Regular Classrooms" revealed that several positive things happened when the visual spatial delivery method was implemented for him in his 7th-grade classroom. What were some of these positive results?
   (grades improved; attitude toward school improved; behavior in classroom improved; frustration was reduced; organizational skills improved; independence increased)
7. As detailed in "Hearing Impaired Students in Regular Classrooms," what are some of the advantages and disadvantages to a regular education teacher of taking the time to prepare materials for a visual delivery of concepts to a hearing impaired student mainstreamed in the class?
   (**advantages:** *student will learn better; student will not be as frustrated and act out his tensions with bad behavior; student will be more interested in materials being presented;* **disadvantages:** *very time-consuming; a challenge for teacher to find a way to visually present many objects, qualities or relations being taught)*
8. The techniques presented in "Hearing Impaired Students in Regular Classrooms" have the potential to help other classifications of handicapped students. What other students might benefit from visual over auditory presentations? Why?
   (learning disabled students with language disabilities because they cannot receive, integrate and express well with spoken words; LD students with auditory-perceptual disorders because they cannot receive and integrate information presented orally; attention-deficit disordered students because their attention span for listening is short; language-disordered students because they have limited vocabularies)

43. "LEAST RESTRICTIVE ENVIRONMENTS" FOR THE DEAF,
JOAN CHAMPIE   AE p. 196

ARTICLE SUMMARY

The author contends that deaf students are entitled to be grouped with peers and taught by trained professionals in classes where they can be challenged but not overwhelmed, using methods and materials designed for their needs. Mainstreamed classes may restrict these rights much more than a state residential institution would.

KEY TERMS AND TOPICS

Least Restrictive Environment an educational setting for an exceptional child which comes as close as possible to a regular classroom, or is a regular classroom.

CRITICAL ANALYSIS

Multiple Choice Questions

1. The author of " 'Least Restrictive Environments' for the Deaf" feels that deaf students need to do all of the following *except:*
   a. gossip in the lavatory.
   b. participate in competitive sports.
   c. elect class officers.
   *d. play a musical instrument.
2. According to " 'Least Restrictive Environments' for the Deaf," deaf students in mainstreamed high school classes may be more restricted than deaf students in state institutions for all of the following reasons *except:*
   a. fewer choices of vocational education courses.
   *b. fewer criteria for appropriateness of IEPs (individualized education programs).
   c. fewer deaf role models.
   d. fewer deaf peers.
3. As explained in " 'Least Restrictive Environments' for the Deaf," PL 94-142 does not provide criteria to protect deaf students in all of the following areas *except:*
   *a. parental participation in the educational planning.
   b. assessment of deaf population base in local districts.
   c. transfer from local districts to state schools.
   d. monitoring of IEP to determine if it is least restrictive.

True/False Questions

4. According to " 'Least Restrictive Environments' for the Deaf," deaf students living in state institutions for the deaf usually have more opportunities for after school, evening, and weekend extracurricular activities in which they can communicate effectively and satisfyingly than do deaf students living in their home districts. (T)
5. " 'Least Restrictive Environments' for the Deaf" reveals that deaf children are usually convinced that they will become blind as well by the time they grow up. (F)

GENERAL QUESTIONS

6. The author of " 'Least Restrictive Environments' for the Deaf" believes legislators and educators should evaluate five areas before determining what is the least restrictive environment for deaf children. What are these specific areas?
   (academics; vocational training opportunities; extracurricular activities available for the deaf; social life; family life)
7. Vocational training for deaf students is very important. According to " 'Least Restrictive Environments' for the Deaf," what are the advantages of getting this training in a state residential institution rather than in a public school? What are the disadvantages?

(**advantages:** *wider selection of vocational courses especially for the deaf; job counseling; supervised on-the-job experiences; deaf role models; post-graduation placement and employment assistance;* **disadvantages:** *little interaction with hearing peers; less frequent interaction with family members*)

8. Based on your reading of " 'Least Restrictive Environments' for the Deaf," should all handicapped students be segregated from their nonhandicapped peers in high school in order to provide intensive vocational training designed for persons with their special classification of exceptionality? For which types of handicapped students would this be more desirable? Less desirable?

(**more desirable:** *deaf; moderately to severely mentally retarded; blind; multihandicapped; emotionally disturbed; some orthopedically handicapped; some health impaired;* **less desirable:** *some orthopedically handicapped; some health impaired; speech impaired; learning disabled; mildly retarded; behaviorally disordered; gifted; hearing impaired; visually impaired*)

44. THE VISUALLY HANDICAPPED CHILD,
WILLIAM V. PADULA AND SUSAN J. SPUNGIN
AE p. 200

ARTICLE SUMMARY

The majority of visually handicapped children are not blind. They may need special help to utilize the vision they have. This article describes the developmental problems that may occur without such help, and urges early diagnosis and training or optical aids when required for the visually impaired infant and young child.

KEY TERMS AND TOPICS

Acuity ability to see clearly.
Field of Vision scope or peripheral extent of sight.
Visually Impaired 20/70 acuity or less in best corrected eye.
Legally Blind 20/200 acuity or less in the best corrected eye, or a 20-degree field of vision or less.
Low Vision Examination differs from a routine visual examination because it determines what can be done beyond conventional glasses.
Low Vision Optical Aids technologies designed to allow low-vision people to utilize the vision they have.

CRITICAL ANALYSIS

Multiple Choice Questions

1. In "The Visually Handicapped Child," which of the following is *not* indicated as a determinant of a vision impaired child's function and development?
   a. other physical abilities.
   b. intelligence.
   c. other environmental surroundings.
   *d. general health.

2. According to "The Visually Handicapped Child," seventy percent of all the sensory nerves in the body come from the eyes and enable humans to do all of the following *except:*
   *a. move.
   b. maintain balance.
   c. think.
   d. see.

3. According to "The Visually Handicapped Child," development in the visually impaired infant may be delayed because:
   a. vision is necessary for normal development.
   b. parental overprotectiveness prevents exploration.
   *c. other sensory-motor functions need time to mature to the point where they can compensate for lack of vision.
   d. intelligence must develop before the child is able to utilize other senses to compensate for lack of vision.

True/False Questions

4. According to "The Visually Handicapped Child," a child with 20/70 visual acuity in the best corrected eye cannot qualify for federal or state funding of special educational services under PL 94-142. (F)

5. "The Visually Handicapped Child" states that the majority of children who are visually handicapped are not blind, but have usable vision. (T)

GENERAL QUESTIONS

6. According to "The Visually Handicapped Child," what might the consequences be by not identifying and compensating for low vision in infancy?
   (*failure to utilize the visual capacities available; consequent delay in developing other capacities, such as coordination, balance, thinking, and problem solving; failure to provide necessary aids; failure or delay in providing appropriate training; misdiagnosis as retarded or otherwise developmentally impaired*)

7. In the article "The Visually Handicapped Child," what is the basic reason visual impairment leads to developmental delay?
   (*active matching of information about the world received through various senses is impaired, leading to delays in developing knowledge of relations among objects*)

8. What are the solutions proposed in "The Visually Handicapped Child" for treating infants and young children who are vision impaired?
   (*visual aids, such as glasses, hand-held magnifiers, telescopes and microscopes; closed circuit TV and special programs designed to maximize vision use through visual stimulation*)

45. MAINSTREAMING CHILDREN WITH VISUAL IMPAIRMENTS,
S.C. ASHCROFT AND A.M. ZAMBONE-ASHLEY
AE p. 203

ARTICLE SUMMARY

The article discusses the history of residential treatment as well as mainstreaming for the visually handicapped, the criteria for various placement options, the wide range of visual impairment conditions and individual needs, and the appropriate use of educational resources.

KEY TERMS AND TOPICS

Partially Sighted "corrected visual acuity of 20/70 or less in the better eye" or the visual field subtends an angle no greater than 140 degrees; also called visually impaired.
Braille Reader a child who can only read Braille.
Print Reader a child who is partially sighted and can read either large or regular print, if necessary, under special conditions.
Mainstreaming educating children with handicaps in regular education programs with supporting help from specially trained personnel.

CRITICAL ANALYSIS

Multiple Choice Questions

1. In "Mainstreaming Children With Visual Impairments," visually impaired children are most likely to differ from others in verbal, conceptual, and social skills primarily due to:
   *a. disadvantage in observing objects and their relations to environment.
   b. decreased amount of reading.
   c. negative attitudes of others.
   d. lack of self-confidence.

2. "Mainstreaming Children With Visual Impairments" suggests that educational settings where a child participates in the integrated classroom, yet receives intensive instruction with

other children with visual limitations in special skills areas, are particularly useful to a child who has all but one of the following traits:
    a. need to develop mobility.
    b. need to develop orientation.
    *c. need to develop social skills.
    d. need to develop Braille reading skills.

True/False Questions

3. As stated in "Mainstreaming Children With Visual Impairments," mainstreaming of blind children did not occur until PL 94-142 was passed in 1975. (F)
4. "Mainstreaming Children With Visual Impairments" states that the "zero reject" philosophy believes that all handicapped children should be entitled to special education in special classes or special schools rather than being placed in regular classrooms. (F)

GENERAL QUESTIONS

5. The authors of "Mainstreaming Children With Visual Impairments" list criteria that need to be met for visually impaired students to function effectively in local schools. Discuss these and describe any others you consider important. *(adequate home situation; textbooks for each subject; equipment and special materials both at home and at school; adequate reader service; a teacher-consultant; opportunity and support for participation in extracurricular activities)*
6. "Mainstreaming Children With Visual Impairments" suggests that the efforts that must be made to integrate a child with visual impairments into a mainstreamed classroom are similar to those required for every new child in the class. Discuss what these efforts are and whether you agree that they are the same for visually impaired and nonhandicapped students. *(introduction to the setting; provision of special materials and equipment; meeting of needs for physical recreation and special activities; attention to social integration; proper adaptation of the curriculum; integration into extracurricular activities; adjustment by teacher to student individuality)*
7. "Mainstreaming Children With Visual Impairments" emphasizes the need to treat the IEP as a flexible and developing plan. What are some of the means urged for developing and improving the plan? *(observation of the student; gathering information about the student; identifying resources in and out of the classroom; listing and priorizating the child's needs; selecting goals; listing appropriate activities to meet them; identifying persons to carry out activities; discussion with child, family, and other teachers; frequent review of plan)*

46. TEACHING PARTIALLY SIGHTED CHILDREN, PATRICIA ANNE DAVIS AE p. 213

ARTICLE SUMMARY

This article, by an itinerant teacher of blind and partially sighted children, is designed for general education teachers who may have partially sighted students. It suggests ways of identifying such children, making classroom work easier for them to follow, evaluating their ability to perform various activities, and adapting the teacher's behavior to their needs.

KEY TERMS AND TOPICS

Partially Sighted Child one who is visually impaired but who can read print, either regular or enlarged.
Educationally Blind children who use Braille.

CRITICAL ANALYSIS
Multiple Choice Questions

1. In the article "Teaching Partially Sighted Children," all of the following were given as characteristics of children who should be referred for vision screening *except:*
    a. avoiding ball games.
    b. copying incorrectly from the chalkboard.
    c. recurrent eye infections.
    *d. holding reading matter far away from face.
2. In the article "Teaching Partially Sighted Children," which of the following is considered potentially dangerous for children with impaired sight?
    a. use of power tools.
    *b. contact sports.
    c. use of matches.
    d. running.
3. In the article "Teaching Partially Sighted Children," which of the following is *not* recommended for teachers working with a partially sighted child?
    a. ask the child's preferences for seating, lighting and size of type.
    *b. call attention to the child's disability so peers will show pity.
    c. meet the child's parents and discuss their expectations and concerns.
    d. try to determine, without asking, if a child is seeing displayed materials.

True/False Questions

4. According to "Teaching Partially Sighted Children," partially sighted children often skip words or lose their place in a book while reading. (T)
5. The author of "Teaching Partially Sighted Children" says that no matter what a mainstream teacher does, a partially sighted child will always seem very different from the other children. (F)

GENERAL QUESTIONS

6. "Teaching Partially Sighted Children" suggests that the emotional needs of partially sighted children are the same as those of all children, but indicates that they may need to be fulfilled in special ways. Indicate what those ways might be. *(private discussion with child about his/her needs; don't call public attention to the child's differences; call the child by name; be aware of signs of unexpressed frustration resulting from inadequate vision)*
7. What functions are recommended for itinerant teachers in "Teaching Partially Sighted Children"? *(assessing visual functioning; determine how to let child use visual capacities as much as possible; supplying special materials and equipment; teaching special skills; counseling the child and parents; liaison to other special services)*
8. What methods are recommended in "Teaching Partially Sighted Children" for the problems visually impaired students face when their classes take tests? *(typed or printed copy of tests given from the board or overhead projector; darkest, clearest copies of test materials; possible reduced quantity, but not quality, of work, in recognition of delays due to difficulty focusing; oral rather than written testing where mechanical difficulties excessively slow the ability to demonstrate other skills and knowledge)*

47. APPROPRIATE EDUCATION FOR VISUALLY HANDICAPPED STUDENTS, GERALDINE T. SCHOLL AE p. 216

ARTICLE SUMMARY

This article explores three questions: What students are visually handicapped? What special needs do they have? What should be included in their IEPs? The author systematically provides answers, emphasizing creative placement practices and special techniques for education.

KEY TERMS AND TOPICS

Heterogeneous Population a population with many differences and many unlike qualities.
Optacon a device which converts images of regular print on the retina of a camera to vibrations of tiny pins in the shape of the letters to enable visually impaired/blind persons to perceive and read the letters with their fingers.

CRITICAL ANALYSIS

Multiple Choice Questions

1. The author of "Appropriate Education for Visually Handicapped Students" emphasized three aspects of education which need to be made more appropriate. Which was not emphasized?
   a. creative placement practices.
   b. individualized education programs.
   *c. parental participation.
   d. assessment procedures.

2. Which appearance of the eyes is not usually associated with visual impairment, according to "Appropriate Education for Visually Handicapped Students"?
   a. inflamed or watery eyes.
   b. crossed eyes.
   *c. unequal dilation of the pupils.
   d. encrusted or swollen eyelids.

3. The author of "Appropriate Education for Visually Handicapped Students" feels that in addition to routine vision screening and a physiological eye examination, a visually impaired child needs to be given a functional vision assessment. Which professional person conducts this assessment?
   *a. a special education teacher.
   b. a school nurse.
   c. an optometrist.
   d. an ophthalmologist.

True/False Questions

4. According to "Appropriate Education for Visually Handicapped Students," visually impaired students compose a homogeneous population with special educational needs which are easily met. (F)

5. As stated in "Appropriate Education for Visually Handicapped Students," many visually impaired students never acquire the concepts of three dimensions and colors. (T)

GENERAL QUESTIONS

6. The author of "Appropriate Education for Visually Handicapped Students" feels that grouping visually impaired pupils for special educational purposes is not possible in most school districts. What are some of the reasons she gives for this?
   (small population; wide range of ages, special needs, visual abilities, and intellectual abilities; need different delivery systems; have different cultural/familial needs; live in wide geographical radius from schools)

7. Visually impaired students usually need substitutes for or supplements to the typical visual materials used in classrooms, such as large print or Braille books, recorded materials, typewriters, an Optacon, volunteer readers, magnifiers and telescopes. According to "Appropriate Education for Visually Handicapped Students," what are the advantages and disadvantages of using these aids in regular classrooms?
   *(**advantages**: impaired student remains in class with non-impaired peers; student challenged to keep up with lessons; student challenged to use residual vision effectively and efficiently; **disadvantages**: impaired student's disability is continually called to attention of others because of special materials or equipment; student may be overwhelmed by pace of regular class as he/she tries to keep up with slower Braille or Optacon reading; no interaction with visually impaired/blind role models)*

8. What are some of the variables mentioned in "Appropriate Education for Visually Handicapped Students" which make visually impaired/blind students, as well as students in every other category of exceptionality, more heterogeneous than homogeneous?
   (age of onset of handicap; degree of and etiology of handicap; presence of other concurrent handicapping conditions; intellectual abilities; attitudes of family; attitudes of school personnel; attitudes of community members; social and cultural characteristics of family)

48. TECHNOLOGY AND THE HANDICAPPED,
JOHN M. WILLIAMS   AE p. 220

ARTICLE SUMMARY

This nontechnical article describes various developments in talking computers, terminals, typewriters, and other high-tech devices. It describes their use for disabled people in educational settings and urges their increased use.

KEY TERMS AND TOPICS

Synthetic Speech speech produced by mechanical combination of sounds.
Synthesizer Board microelectronic equipment used for producing synthetic speech.
Phonemes a sound that distinguishes one utterance from another, such as "th" and "sh" and long and short vowels.

CRITICAL ANALYSIS

Multiple Choice Questions

1. According to the article "Technology and the Handicapped," computers are now being used not only to help the blind but also:
   a. the physically abused.
   b. the emotionally disturbed.
   *c. the learning disabled.
   d. the health impaired.

2. One of the technical advances of computers that is especially useful to blind students, according to "Technology and the Handicapped," is:
   a. word processing.
   *b. synthetic speech.
   c. graphic production.
   d. image analysis.

3. In the article "Technology and the Handicapped," all but which of the following is described as a goal of research on computer applications for the handicapped?
   a. computer tutoring for drill and practice.
   b. teaching skills for a career in computer technology.
   c. using the equipment in computer literacy courses.
   *d. use of computers to allow improved mobility for visually handicapped.

True/False Questions

4. According to "Technology and the Handicapped," the Council for Exceptional Children is a strong advocate for the use of synthetic speech in all educational grades. (T)

5. "Technology and the Handicapped" states that the federal government is exploring ways to use high technology in educational delivery systems and is both promoting and funding research in this area. (T)

GENERAL QUESTIONS

6. The author of "Technology and the Handicapped" argues the advantages of using computers to help the disabled. What uses does he indicate and what future uses could you envision?
   (current uses include providing computerized information through speech, allowing those who cannot speak to communicate via computer; immediate machine feedback on student performance given verbally; and providing information from analog instruments verbally)

7. What are some of the features recommended for talking computers in the article "Technology and the Handicapped"?
   (good speech quality; user definable speech; intelligent terminal capabilities; information retrieval capability; languages used; storage; disk drives used; and ability to produce Braille)

8. The article "Technology and the Handicapped" urges the expanded use of talking computers in education settings. What might be the problems that would have to be dealt with in

introducing such equipment into normal mainstreamed classrooms?
(cost and protection of equipment; proper training of teachers; sound conflict; attitudes of other students; securing proper material for use on the computers; integrating such material into normal classroom procedures)

49. CHILDREN ON MEDICATION: A GUIDE FOR TEACHERS,
CAROLYN N. LINDSEY, SUSAN R. LEIBOLD,
FRANCES T. LADD, AND RALPH OWNBY   **AE p. 226**

ARTICLE SUMMARY
This is a brief presentation of some of the issues raised for teachers by the mainstreaming of handicapped students who may be taking medication for their conditions. It is accompanied by an extensive chart listing various drugs, their reasons for use, the conditions for which they are used, and side effects that may be noticed by teachers.

KEY TERMS AND TOPICS
Theophylline Preparations tablets or elixirs which relax bronchial walls to reduce the wheezing of an asthma attack.
Side Effects effects, usually undesirable, which result from drug administration in addition to the desired therapeutic effects.

CRITICAL ANALYSIS
Multiple Choice Questions

1. In the article "Children on Medication," side effects of a theophylline preparation may make children exhibit all but which of the following symptoms?
   a. restlessness.
   *b. fatigue.
   c. inability to concentrate.
   d. inability to settle down.
2. The authors of "Children on Medication" suggest that teachers not only learn about drugs and their effects and side effects from articles such as this, but that they also ask all of the following persons about the child's idiosyncratic response to the drug, *except:*
   a. the child.
   b. the child's parents.
   c. the child's physician.
   *d. the pharmacist who supplies the drug to the child.
3. According to "Children on Medication," serious side effects of drugs taken by handicapped students:
   *a. may sometimes be alleviated by additional drugs.
   b. should be ignored by the teacher.
   c. may require placement changes for the student.
   d. are usually only temporary.

True/False Questions

4. The chart given in the article "Children on Medication" is comprehensive and quickly provides all the information a teacher needs to know about each drug. (F)
5. According to "Children on Medication," some parents are unaware of the side effects of the prescription drug(s) their child takes and do not realize that the child's behavior is different because of the drug(s). (T)

GENERAL QUESTIONS

6. What advantages are suggested in "Children on Medication" as likely to flow from a teacher's knowledge of a student's medication and its side effects?
   (the teacher knows what to expect; can assist the child; can work with therapeutic team to eliminate unnecessary problems)
7. What negative effects may a concerned but uninformed teacher have on students who are hyperactive as a result of medication, according to "Children on Medication"?

(may exert inappropriate pressure for better performance; provide more structure in classroom; punish students by withholding privileges; send students to counselor)
8. According to "Children on Medication," what side effects of drugs taken by a handicapped child might be misinterpreted by teachers as a sign of illness, and how might such misinterpretation affect the children?
   (vomiting, loss of appetite, lethargy, fatique; if students are unaware of drug-related cause, they may think that they are sick or worry that they are not exerting enough effort and therefore feel guilty)

50. IS THERE A CHILD WITH EPILEPSY IN THE CLASSROOM?
HAZEL ZAKARIASEN   **AE p. 229**

ARTICLE SUMMARY
Approximately four million Americans and about one in every 50 schoolchildren have epilepsy. This article, directed toward teachers, discusses the nature of epilepsy, some of the signs a teacher may observe, and proper attitudes and behaviors for teachers with epileptic students.

KEY TERMS AND TOPICS
Epilepsy a dysfunction of electrical impulses emitted by the brain.
Petit Mal Epilepsy "absence seizures" that last for just a few seconds and appear similar to daydreaming.
Psychomotor Epilepsy marked by complex partial seizures, such as longer staring spells, involuntary movements or twitches by one body part, or sleepwalk-type movement.
Grand Mal Epilepsy seizures in which the person falls and the whole body convulses, saliva runs from the mouth, and there is possible loss of bladder control.

CRITICAL ANALYSIS
Multiple Choice Questions

1. Which of the following should a teacher do for a student who has a grand mal seizure, according to "Is There a Child with Epilepsy in the Classroom?"
   a. restrain the child to prevent injury.
   b. put a piece of cardboard in the child's mouth to prevent biting the tongue.
   *c. remove any nearby hard or sharp object by which the child might be harmed.
   d. call a doctor immediately.
2. According to "Is There a Child with Epilepsy in the Classroom?" if a child engages in sleep-walk type movement and appears to have involuntary movement of a body part, he or she may be having which type of epileptic seizure?
   a. petit mal.
   *b. psychomotor.
   c. grand mal.
   d. Jacksonian.
3. According to "Is There a Child with Epilepsy in the Classroom?" epileptic students can participate in all normal school activities with the possible exception of:
   *a. contact sports.
   b. emotionally stressful activities.
   c. physically fatiguing activities.
   d. work that involves eyestrain.

True/False Questions

4. According to "Is There a Child with Epilepsy in the Classroom?" epilepsy can happen to anyone, at any period of life. (T)
5. Epilepsy, asserts "Is There a Child with Epilepsy in the Classroom?" is a form of an infectious disease. (F)

6. What does the author of "Is There a Child with Epilepsy in the Classroom?" suggest as ways to overcome society's negative feelings about epilepsy?
   (public exposure such as that given by the Kennedy and Humphrey families to mental retardation; recognition of the great figures past and present who have had epilepsy; reducing mystery associated with the disease through factual information; recognition of the changes resulting from the ability to control epilepsy effectively with medication)
7. What does the article "Is There a Child with Epilepsy in the Classroom?" encourage teachers to convey to their classes regarding epilepsy?
   (information about what epilepsy is and is not; understanding that a seizure is temporary and does not hurt; a matter-of-fact attitude that the seizure is no more important than any ordinary childhood illness)
8. What activities does the article "Is There a Child with Epilepsy in the Classroom?" suggest that teachers can become involved in outside the classroom which may help epileptic students?
   (work with the family in a supportive way; become an advocate for better understanding among educators and the public; stand ready to vouch for capabilities of epileptic students with prospective employers; be a liaison between persons or families affected by epilepsy)

51. YOUNG, INNOCENT AND PREGNANT,
ELIZABETH STARK   AE p. 233

ARTICLE SUMMARY

One out of every ten teenage girls in the United States becomes pregnant every year and about one half of these pregnancies are carried to term. Pregnancy creates health risks, some physical limitations and many educational problems. The author discusses ways to ease these problems.

KEY TERMS AND TOPICS

Contraception something which prevents the conception of offspring by preventing the union of an ovum and a sperm.

CRITICAL ANALYSIS
Multiple Choice Questions

1. All of the following were given as reasons why teenage girls do not use contraception in the article "Young, Innocent and Pregnant" *except:*
   a. ambivalence about sexual activity.
   b. too embarrassed to get contraceptive aids.
   c. denial of the possibility that sex may occur.
   *d. too expensive to purchase contraceptive aids.
2. The author of "Young, Innocent and Pregnant" states that school-based clinics that provide health services, including contraceptive counseling, are usually staffed by all of the following professionals *except:*
   a. social workers.
   *b. pastoral counselors.
   c. physicians.
   d. nurses.
3. According to "Young, Innocent and Pregnant," which of the following is *not* typical of children born to young teenage mothers?
   a. they are born prematurely or with low birthweight.
   b. they are supported by the mother only, often at poverty level.
   c. they have lower IQs than children born to older mothers.
   *d. they are put up for adoption.

True/False Questions

4. According to "Young, Innocent and Pregnant," the older teenagers are when they initiate sexual activity, the more likely they will be to use contraceptives. (T)
5. According to "Young, Innocent and Pregnant," teenagers who are behind academically in school are about three times more likely to become unwed parents than are academic achievers. (T)

6. Several reasons why teenage girls may become pregnant, besides the failure to use birth control, were suggested in "Young, Innocent and Pregnant." What are some of these?
   (to have a baby to love; to get needed attention; to entrap a reluctant suitor; to assert their independence from their parents; to become their mother's equal; to keep up with pregnant girlfriend; to please boyfriend)
7. What does the author of "Young, Innocent and Pregnant" suggest that educators teach or do to help reduce the incidence of teenage pregnancy?
   (begin courses on sex and sexuality at earlier ages; establish school links with family planning clinics; establish school-based health clinics which have many health services, including contraceptive counseling; get local television stations to air messages about birth control; teach assertiveness and skills in saying "no" to sexual activity; increase teenagers' self-esteem; increase hopes that vocational training will provide success in working world)
8. According to "Young, Innocent and Pregnant," why do young teenage mothers produce proportionately more children with handicapping conditions such as mental retardation, learning disabilities, neurological defects, emotional disorders, or multihandicaps?
   (have little or no prenatal care; have nutrient-poor diets during pregnancy; have premature births; have low birth-weight infants; provide inadequate diets to infants; may physically abuse or neglect their infants; provide very little cognitive or social stimulation for their infants)

52. COMPREHENSIVE MICROCOMPUTER APPLICATIONS FOR SEVERELY HANDICAPPED CHILDREN,
G. EVAN RUSHAKOFF AND LINDA J. LOMARDINO
                                                     AE p. 237

ARTICLE SUMMARY

The authors describe the current use of microcomputers for severely physically handicapped children, present several case histories, evaluate existing hardward and software, and suggest considerations to keep in mind when deciding on computer aids to particular handicapped individuals.

KEY TERMS AND TOPICS

Keyboard Adaptations modifications in the way the user instructs the computer.
Single Switch Programs computer software or hardware under which all letter or number characters are arranged horizontally on the bottom of the screen and a pointer or marker performs a step-scan process from left to right across the characters until the switch is activated to indicate a desired entry.
Adaptive Firmware Card allows single and multiple switch control of all Apple programs.
Interactive Software provides stimulus, prompting, feedback and reinforcement to users.

CRITICAL ANALYSIS
Multiple Choice Questions

1. In the article "Comprehensive Microcomputer Applications for Severely Handicapped Children," what advantage is stated for educational programs which possess the capability to maintain ongoing data?
   a. student can recheck work to find errors.
   *b. student's work can be monitored immediately or in the future.
   c. student can find place if lost.
   d. record of accomplishment can be maintained.

2. According to "Comprehensive Microcomputer Applications for Severely Handicapped Children," all but which of the following recreational programs are appropriate for severely physically impaired children?
   a. games of strategy.
   b. games of memory.
   c. games of logic.
   *d. arcade games.
3. "Comprehensive Microcomputer Applications for Severely Handicapped Children" states that microcomputers can produce communication in all of the following ways *except:*
   a. printed material.
   b. monitor display.
   *c. recorded speech.
   d. synthesized speech.

True/False Questions

4. According to "Comprehensive Microcomputer Applications for Severely Handicapped Children," computer software has now been developed to allow physically impaired children to sculpt as well as compose music and produce flat artwork. (F)
5. According to "Comprehensive Microcomputer Applications for Severely Handicapped Children," very few computer programs require reading skills, so they are very appropriate for severely retarded children as well as physically handicapped children. (F)

GENERAL QUESTIONS

6. Why does the article "Comprehensive Microcomputer Applications for Severely Handicapped Children" suggest that microcomputers may improve the self-concept of physically impaired students?
   (increased sense of autonomy through reduced dependence on others; allows children to affect and control their world; a tool with which they can become proficient and show their creativity; allows them to see themselves as learners and doers)
7. What considerations does "Comprehensive Microcomputer Applications for Severely Handicapped Children" urge be kept in mind in prescribing a microcomputer as a comprehensive living aid for the physically impaired child?
   (reading ability; involvement of all caregivers in decision; primary caregivers' involvement in goal setting; adaptation to stationary character of computer)
8. What are some of the features of microcomputers which make them useful as communications aids for the severely physically handicapped, according to "Comprehensive Microcomputer Applications for Severely Handicapped Children"?
   (ability to communicate in several modes; increase in speed over other communication aids; ability to communicate orally; ability to communicate in speech to those not familiar with sign or other specialized modes)

THE
BOOK
PHONE™
800-243-6532

For information pertaining to our publications
please call the Sales Service Group
203-453-4351 (In Canada call collect)

The Dushkin Publishing Group, Inc., Sluice Dock, Guilford, Connecticut 06437
ISBN: 0-87967-706-6